TRIBAL DANCE AND SONGS

CASTES AND TRIBES OF INDIA-SERIES

1. Continuity and Change Among the Ahom/ **Nitul Kumar Gogai**
2. Ethnography of a Nomadic Tribe: A Study of Yanadi/ **N. Sudhakar Rao**
3. Mythos and Logos of the Warlis: A Tribal World View/ **Ajay Dandekar (Ed)**
4. Naga Cultural Attires and Musical Instruments/ **A. Lanu Ao (Ed.)**
5. Socio-Cultural Study of Scheduled Tribes: The Pardhans of Maharashtra/ **S.R. Murkute**
6. The Banjara/ **S.G. Deogaonkar** and **Shailaja S. Deogaonkar**
7. The Kolam Tribals/ **S.G. Deogaonkar** and **Leena Deogaonkar Baxi**
8. The Korku Tribals/ **S.G. Deogaonkar** and **Shailaja S. Deogaonkar**
9. Tribal Dance and Songs/ **S.G. Deogaonkar** and **Shailaja S. Deogaonkar**

About the Authors

Dr. S.G. Deogaonkar a retired Reader in Political Science, holding Master Degrees in Political Science and Public Administration and a Ph.D. degree in Social Science. He also holds an LL.M. degree in Constitutional Law. A scholar of repute, he has completed about ten post-doctoral research projects and has about fifteen books to his credit based on his research, mostly based on field-work.

Dr. Deogaonkar specialises in Political Anthropology and Tribal Development. For the last fifteen years he was a Non-official Member in the Governing Council of the Tribal Research & Training Institute. Maharashtra State (Pune) and for ten years was Member of the Zonal Advisory Council for the Western Zone of the Life Insurance Corporation of India. Till recently, he was Member of the Expert Committee appointed by the Maharashtra State for re-verification of entries of Tribal communities in the State Governments Resolution of 1985.

Some of his reputed books include, The Madia of Bhamragad, The Korku Tribals, The Banjara, The Hill Korwa, Tribal Exploitation, Tribal Development Plans; etc.

Dr. (Mrs.) S.S. Deogaonkar holds a Masters degree in Language and a Ph.D. in Tribal Linguistics and Folk-literature. She has been teaching degree classes in Colleges affiliated to the Nagpur University on contributory basis. She specialises in tribal linguistics and tribal folk-literature and was awarded Best Literature Award for the year 1990-91 by the Maharashtra State for her book on the Madia dialect. She has collected and documented tribal folk-songs and folk-tales and has published many books in Marathi and English. She was a member of the State Level Committee on District Primary Education Programme (DPEP) and a Resource person for Training Programmes for teachers working in tribal area organised by the State Council for Educational Research and Training.

TRIBAL DANCE AND SONGS

S.G. DEOGAONKAR
SHAILAJA S. DEOGAONKAR

CONCEPT PUBLISHING COMPANY PVT. LTD.
NEW DELHI-110059

ISBN: 978-81-8069-010-5

First Published 2003

Published and Printed by

Concept
Since 1974

Concept Publishing Company Pvt. Ltd.
A/15-16, Commercial Block, Mohan Garden,
New Delhi-110059 (India)
T: 91-11-41101460
E: publishing@conceptpub.com, *W*: www.conceptpub.com

Preface

Many monographs and books on different tribal communities have come out during the last fifty years. The present authors have also contributed quite a few titles to the series. Very often the contents are ethnographic and give information about the tribe, its culture, social organisation, developmental status, economic problems including exploitation and so on. However a very important part of tribal culture and tribal genre, namely their folk-literature is often neglected. It may hardly be covered in a chapter or so, which is also rarely done. Due to development and modernisation, the new generations from the tribal communities are forgetting their tribal dialects, folk-literature etc. very fast.

A few old persons, the 'learned informants', may also become extinct in near future. Like the tribal knowledge of the traditional herbal medicine, the folk literature — mainly consisting of tribal folk-songs — may also slowly pass out into obscurity. This indicates the need for collection, documentation and preservation of this rich treasure of tribal literature which is also — in a very true sense — the mirror of tribal culture. Audio as well as Video Cassettes may be used for this purpose, however so as to know the pronunciation of the words and to know the meaning of the words, it is essential to put it in print form. Our mentor and guide in studies on tribal populations, late Prof. Christoph Von Furer-Haimendorf had opined at our U.G.C. Seminar held in a Gond village Wangepalli (near Aheri in Gadchiroli district) during 1978-79 that for the transcription of all Indian tribal dialects, *Devnagari* is the only perfect script. Though we adopted this view for reducing the songs collected from tribal dialects to print, with a view to reach this treasure of traditional tribal folklore to international audience we have tried here to present the folk literature of tribes in Roman script, in a collective and rather comparative form.

The pages that follow will show that the literary values of tribal folk literature are really very high and may be compared to that found in languages of advanced communities. The sentiments expressed and the relationships discernible in all tribes (maybe ethnically distant) are not only similar but are closer to our sentiments in our modern world. We hope, this evidence of a common undercurrent of sentiments and culture running through all the so-called primitive and modern people will serve the cause of national integration.

We are extremely grateful to all those who helped us during our fieldwork in different tribes but would like to mention a few names like late Mr. Vasantrao Patwardhan, his son Mohan, Miss Nanda Kulsange from Aheri, Shri Kawdu Nanaji Khapne from Etapalli, Shri Bodanga Kando, Manohar and Bajirao Hichami and Katia Patel from Krishnar (Etapalli), Shri Gogga Pungati, Gaita of Gotpadi (Bhamragad) (all Madias), Shri Arjun Jade Patel *alias* Arjun Guruji — a Korku *Bhumka* from Dahenda (Dharni – Melghat – Dist. Amravati), and Shri Sonare of Toranwadi who worked as our investigator. Shri Shriram Zode, a young Kolam graduate and his Kolam friends helped in our fieldwork in the Yavatmal and Chandrapur districts among the Kolams and Pardhans. Shri Laxman Rathod and his Banjara friends helped in collecting folk literature from the Banjaras in Yavatmal district. We thank all of them for their cooperation.

Before we end we must thank Shri Sandeepsingh Thakur who did the work of assistance in preparing the manuscript and drew figures and Shri Genulal Dohade who typed the script.

Last but not the least we thank the Concept Publishing Company, New Delhi for publishing this book in an attractive form.

Warora
Dist. Chandrapur
26th January 2003

S.G. Deogaonkar
Shailaja S. Deogaonkar

Contents

List of Plates

1

Introduction

The tribal folk literature has come to us by an oral tradition. It has been preserved for generations and transferred to the new generations. For any oral transmission poetic form is best because it can be easily remembered and reproduced. The tribal tradition is also based on dancing and singing to the tunes of music. It is very often observed that the tribal men and women first start dancing, with music based primarily on rhythm and then only they start singing the songs. The music also is based on the various natural tunes, notes, and chords which they come across in Nature. The sounds of the birds and wild animals, the sounds of the rivers and waves of winds are the sources of their music. Consequently many of the words in their music are onomatopoeic. Similarly their poetry is in a real sense a spontaneous overflow of emotions because due to their natural environment they are more responsive and sensitive to the stimulate from Nature. The joy and ecstasy which results due to their response to Nature flows out in the form of poetry. Most of the natural phenomena observed in Nature are reflected in their songs.

The tribal folk songs are sung only while dancing (They are not accustomed to sing while sitting) and hence these songs should be correctly called as 'Dancing-songs'. One may say that their songs are not 'sung' but are 'danced'. Dances are very common and is a matter of daily routine. All occasions in personal and social life are celebrated with dancing. Right from the birth-ritual, to marriage or even in death rituals dancing and singing are very common. On festivals during farming, while doing labour work in forest or elsewhere songs are sung and dances are danced. Most of the tribals possess the skill of composing poems briskly, befitting the occasion. Similarly many folk-tales are also contained in the songs. Thus tribal folk literature is mainly found in their songs and the singing and dancing is traditionally a collective or a community affair.

The tribal people are experts in the performing arts specially the folk-drama. They have developed different art forms the most common of which are, Dandar, Ramlila, and specialise in dance befitting the occasion, for example, the *Khamm* dance of the Korku, the *Ghusadi* dance of the Kolam, the *Rela* or the *Dussera* dances of the Madia etc. They have their own methods of makeup, developed indigenously from locally available natural material like stones and soils, resins from the trees, animal skins and feathers of the birds. Their musical instruments like drums (*Dhol*) of different types, flutes, trumpets etc. are also locally prepared. Of late, they have adopted modern musical instruments like Harmonium, *Ghungroos* of brass and so on.

At the time of dancing and singing two things are very commonly observed, the bon-fire by burning firewood, and consumption of liquor. The Mahua or the Toddy liquors are very common. These give them the necessary vigour or enthusiasm necessary for the strenuous performance.

For the tribals, singing and dancing are collective endeavours. This means that there is no audience as such, because the whole community participates in singing and dancing. Even the songs which are mostly composed on the spur of the moment are either of individual authorship or communal authorship. Mostly one person initiates the line which is then repeated by the whole group. Similarly for setting the tune, rhythm or chord of the music one person leads, and others follow suit. The metre also changes depending upon the song.

The tribal folk literature consists of traditional songs, tales, ritual dramas, question and answer songs, sayings, and even *mantras* and abuses. Songs may be for men, for women or for both which are sung by a mixed group. Lulling songs are also very common. Songs conveying the past history of the community, their origin, social organisation and the great deeds of dead forefathers are also very common, e.g. the *Dhemsa* songs sung by the Pardhans on their traditional instruments '*Kingri*' or '*Bana*' are full of the history of the Gonds and the Pardhans. The Banjara, which is a nomadic tribe from Vidarbha have also many songs which convey the glorious deeds of their forefathers who migrated from Rajasthan. Ritual songs are full of the praise of their Gods and Goddesses and of local deities. The festival songs, particularly to be sung at Holi and Dussera are full of joy, love, and other fine aspects of life. Even the tunes for these songs are different. Songs for sad occasions are altogether different and pathetic. It is also common to find spiritual orientation in some songs which tell us of the futility of earthly life. They have even adopted some Bhajanas from the Saints which are common in the non-tribal population in the vicinity.

A new class of modern songs seems to have cropped and entered the treasure of tribal folk literature. These are pertaining to education and the effects of the education on new generation, development schemes, elections etc. Songs welcoming the guests are composed while dancing before the guest and may include information about the guest. In many tribal songs references to market (Bazaar) and purchases from the market are very common. Traditionally the songs show knowledge about higher metals like silver, gold and the ornaments prepared from these things.

The tribal literature displays tradition as well as change and the adaptability shown is really amazing. Similarly the skill in coining words for ideas and new concepts or in a straightaway adopting words or concepts from the outside mainstream culture in their dialect and folk literature is worth appreciating. Probably it is this quality which has kept the stream or flow of their oral literature continuous and it still exists in spite of the great historical and developmental changes engulfing their populations.

A Brief Introduction to the Tribes

The Gonds

The Gonds form one of the largest tribal population in India and are spread over a sprawling expanse of the subcontinent covering. Central India, and predominantly in Madhya Pradesh, Maharashtra, Andhra Pradesh, etc. They are concentrated in the Chandrapur and Gadchiroli districts of Maharashtra and the Bastar and Adilabad districts of Madhya Pradesh and Andhra Pradesh respectively. In the Gadchiroli district four sub-tribes of Gonds are found, namely the Raj-Gonds, Mādia -Gonds, Dhurve-Gonds and the Khatulwar-Gonds.

The Madia-Gonds, also called the *Madia* or *Mārhiya* are classified as a primitive tribe in Gadchiroli district as socially and economically they are at a lower level of acculturation. The Madia are further sub-divided into Bada-Madia normally living on the hills and the Chota-Madia who have migrated to the forests on the plains.

The Gonds are a Dravidian tribe and as such the Gondi dialect is grouped in the Dravidian languages and shows strong influence of Telugu and Kannada languages. The Madia-Gondi is the original form of dialect and the Gondi is the modified form showing influences from the social environment and adopting words from Hindi, Marathi etc. However, the main structure remains the same. Gondi has a rich treasure of folk literature which is preserved through an oral tradition.

The Pardhans

The Pardhans are ethnically related to the Gonds and have similar social organisation, scheme of Gods and deities and speak the Gondi language. Many anthropologists have called them minstrel of the Gonds. The Gond mythology is preserved by them and they know the religious songs [the Dhemsa(s)] which they sing as lyrical poems on their traditional stringed instruments called *Kingri* or *Bana*. In fact in all Gond marriages and for some rituals a Pardhan singer is a must, though they are treated as a lower caste by Gonds.

The Pardhans are primarily concentrated in the Yavatmal district of Maharashtra and are also found in the Chandrapur and Gadchiroli districts.

The Kolam

The Kolam are also an ethnically related tribe of the Gonds and have similar social organisation, including clan-system, scheme of Gods, etc. Some rituals are also common. In Maharashtra the Kolam are classified as a primitive tribe and are concentrated in Yavatmal, Nanded and Osmanabad districts. They are also found in Adilabad district of Andhra Pradesh. About sixty years ago some Kolams from the Yavatmal and Adilabad districts migrated to the Chandrapur district of Maharashtra. Some Kolams are also found in the Aheri and Sironcha sub-divisions of Gadchiroli district and have preserved the Gond mythology.

Kolami which is their dialect is from the Dravidian group of languages and simulates Gondi in many respects. Many Hindi and Marathi words have been adopted. Gaon-Bandhni is an important ritual of the Kolam and the Ghusadi dance performed on the occasion is well-known. The tribe is economically backward and mostly do stone-breaking or other labour. Their Panchayat system is still functioning very well.

The Korku

The tribe is ethnically related to the other large tribal group, *i.e.* the Munda. They speak Korku dialect which is from the Munda or Kherwarian (or Kolarian) group of languages. It has a strong influence of Nemadi (Nemari) Hindi and they have also adopted a few words from the languages in the vicinity like Marathi. The Korku are concentrated in the Melghat region (Dharni and Chikhaldara tehṣils) of Amravati district in Maharashtra and have spread over the Nemad and Betul districts of Madhya Pradesh.

The social organisation, scheme of Gods etc. is altogether different from that of the Gond tribes. The level of acculturation is also different and they have adopted many things from the adjoining mainstream culture. The Korku call themselves as *Ravan Vanshi* and worship Ravana (the mythological King of Lanka), his son Meghnad and his brother Kumbhakarna. However they also worship Hindu Gods like Hanuman, Shrikrishna, Shri Ram, Ganesh etc. *Khamm* is their ritual dance which is a worship of Lord Shrikrishna and the songs are very popular. The Korku folk-songs are rich in their content as well as have high literary values.

The Banjara

This is a nomadic tribe (classified as *Vimukta Jali* in Maharashtra) having its ethnic origin in Rajputana. Its origin is considered to be from the Aryan race. During the era of Muslim invasion and during famines they seem to have migrated to the South either as carriers or suppliers of foodgrains or as traders. In Maharashtra the Banjara are concentrated in the Yavatmal district and particularly in the Pusad, Darwha and Pandharkawda taluqas of the district. Spillovers are found in other districts of Vidarbha and Marathwada regions. They speak Banjari dialect which sounds to be a mixture of Rajasthani, Marvadi and Hindi. Many Marathi words have also been adopted. The Banjara worship the Banjara Devi, other regional Goddesses like the Renuka Devi at Mahur-Gad, Lord Mahadeo, Shrikrishna and Vitthal (incarnation of Lord Shrikrishna at Pandharpur in Maharashtra), Shriram and Sita etc.

Though originally nomads, they have settled down at many places and do farming, animal husbandry and other occupations though a majority of them subsists on labour work. The tribe is at a very high level of acculturation and provided Chief Ministers, Deputy Chief Ministers and Class I Officers to the State.

However the tribal culture has been largely maintained. The clan system based on their traditional social organisation still persists. The Banjara dances are very colourful and folk-songs reflect their culture and traditions. For all lifecycle rituals and festivals they have songs and dances. The brave deeds of their forefathers, certain customs like bride-price are also observed like those in other tribal communities. Thus, though, ethnologically this nomadic tribe falls apart from the rest of the tribes covered above, so far as the richness of folk-songs, dances and music are concerned they are similar to the other major tribes from Vidarbha region of Maharashtra state.

2

Tribal Dances

The dancing tradition of the tribals is ancient, but has been in vogue till today. One historian named Aaren who accompanied Alexander the Great has also noted the dancing art of the Gonds and rated it as best. Pt. Jawaharlal Nehru took keen interest and appreciated it as one of the classical performing arts of the tribals.

How the dancing art originated is a question which has been answered differently. One of the interpretations found in Gond folk-tales relates to the famous Lingo legend. One of the first social reformers and religious messengers was Pahadi Kupar Lingo. He liberated the Gondi people from the cave, which is located near Salekasa, Darekasa (near the present Gondia Railway Station — about 1 km. away on the southern side) and became their Guru (Preacher). He started giving sermons to them. Once, his disciples were going for taking bath in the river. On the way there were many fragrant flowers. A big black bee was moving around the flowers in circles and producing a sound like 'Roon s s s s s Roon s s s s s Roon s s s . . . .' The Gond disciples were so attracted and possessed by the scene and the sound that they also started moving in circles and reproducing the same sound. Due to this, they were late in taking bath and returned to the place where Lingo was delivering the sermons. When Lingo asked them the reason for coming late, they described the scene which they had seen. Lingo was also attracted and he along with them started dancing and producing the same sound. This is how the Gonds were introduced to the art of dancing. That is why the Gonds dance in circles and all their songs start with syllables related to 'Roon s s ...' like

'Rena s s s . Rena s s . . . Rena . . . .' *or* 'Reelo s s . Rello s s . Reelo s s . Ree s Reelo s s .' *or* 'Relaan s s . Relaan s s Re'.

The place where Lingo used to deliver his sermons was the 'Gotul' and hence the place for dancing and singing also was the 'Gotul'. It was Lingo who gave cultural education to the Gonds and developed their dancing art.

It is also said that the Gonds once saw a Peacock dancing to please the female peacock. The beautiful dance attracted the Gonds and they learnt the dancing art from the peacock. They believe that the God came in the form of peacock to teach them to dance.

A folk-tale of the Baiga tribals tells that once their forefathers saw a tiger beating a drum, a leopord blowing a trumpet and a peacock dancing to the tunes and rhythm of this music. Since then their forefathers started dancing.

Description of a Few Dances

The Dhemsa and Gondi Dances

The Gonds and the Kolams (and also the Pardhans) sing the Dhemsas which are ritual songs narrating the tales about their tribe, forefathers, Deities, etc. Traditionally sixteen Dhemsa songs are sung and when the community celebrates a festival, they dance and sing these songs. In the Hindu month of *Poush*, on a full moon day the ritual is performed. All the men and women dance for pleasing God Persapen. The Dhols of big size are the main instruments for this dance. One person who is the leader of this dancing group takes initiative and holds a flag at the loft of a long stick. Two Dhol beaters beat the Dhols with sticks. The movements and footsteps are very soft and rhythmic.

The men and women put on typical dresses. The women wear saree upto the knees and keep the part above the waist (bosom) uncovered. They put on profuse silver ornaments and flowers and ribbons on the head. Musical bells are put on, around the feet, *i.e.* in the form of anklet, around the waist, etc. Garlands of flowers are put around the neck. The men-folk put on a loin cloth or a short dhoti and take *gonde* (tassels) in their hands. The chief dancer puts on a crown of peacock feathers on his head, has musical bells around his waist and garlands of flower around the neck. The rhythmic movement of the hands and feet of all the dancers are most thrilling.

In some cases just as a traditional costume the barks of the trees or animal skin may be put around the waist and straps of white ash drawn on the body. In some cases short wooden sticks (Tiprya) may be borne in hands which are tossed on the rhythm. This is also called a Dandar as they carry *Dandas* in hands while dancing.

Lezim dance is also performed by some Gonds and Kolam tribals from the Kinwat tehsil of Nanded district. This indicates better acculturisation because lezim is a modern instrument borrowed from non-tribal culture. Duff, a typical type of instrument is used for rhythm.

Kingri, a typical instrument simulating violin is used by the Gonds and Kolams but particularly by the Pardhans who are called the minstrels of the Gonds. The Pardhan who plays on this instrument is called a *Thoti*. He sings the songs about their forefathers while playing on this instrument.

Wind instruments like blow pipe or its modifications may also be added at the time of dance.

Among the Kolams a typical dance which is performed on the occasion of *Gaon bandhani* is called Ghusadi dance.

The *Relaa* s s dance of the Madia-Gonds is also very famous.

Ghorpadi Dance

The Kolams have a typical dance which is called Gghorpadi (a large Lizard or Iguana) dance. This is extremely difficult and based on the movements of an animal which forms a relished dish of this tribe. The dancer puts on just a short dhoti and the rest of the body is uncovered. He crawls on the earth on his palms and toes of the feet, thus imitating the lizard. The musical bells in his feet give out musical chimes. The music is supplied by others playing on the Dhol, Duff and flute. Others dance around the man imitating the lizard. The men and women dancers who put on flowers, peacock feathers and hold bright coloured pieces of cloth in their hands, dance in circles around the centre and those who play on instrument stand at the centre of the circle. When the Dhol beater changes the rhythm the dancers also change their style of dancing.

Dress and Attire Costume

Food shelter and clothing are traditionally considered as the basic necessities of human society. According to the environment and the climate these necessities go on changing.

While those who are from hot climates need minimum dress, those from cold or very cold climate need to dress profusely and heavily. During the primitive stage the bark of trees and leaves were used to cover the bodies. In most of the Central Indian and South Indian tribes the traditional dress was scanty, while in the Himalayan tribes the traditional dress was very heavy and usually of bright colours. In the tribes like the Gonds, only a loin cloth (*Langotee*) used to be put on, but with contacts with the modern civilised society they adopted cloth and clothing or dress. Thus the five metre saree (*Lugda*) for the woman was introduced quite late. Covering the breast either with one end of the saree or by putting on blouse came still late and as yet it has not become a part of tradition. Modern educated girls and boys are now imitating their counter parts from the civilised world and adopting the new dress material as well as the dress forms. However, during rituals, festivals, dancing or performing the traditional folk arts they still put on different attires and costumes displaying their imagination and culture.

In the Kolams while performing the Ghusadi dance, the Ghusadis put on deer skin around the waist. Other people participating in the dance put on attires of Gods and Goddesses befitting the theme of the dance. Bright coloured sarees, blouses are also commonly used, showing that the modern adoptions are finding places in the traditional folk arts. Different types of head gears are put on the head which may include turbans, handkerchiefs, peacock feather, feathers of birds, masks from pulp and so on. Apart from attire, ash, soil and different colours are used to draw stripes on the body, or on the face which gives a different impression and looks like an attire. Various masks are also used to supplement these attires.

Of late, towels, lungis, shawls, half pants are also used for dressing. Normally, the costumes or attire are relevant to the theme of the ritual or dance.

For example, if Gods like Ganesh or Hanuman are to be depicted the attire and the mask will be the different, while if a demon is to be depicted the attire is altogether different.

Not only the dress but even the style of putting on the dress differs from tribe to tribe and also as per occasion. Among the Gonds the women fold the sarees above the knee and one leg is left open from the back side while the Pardhan women put on the saree in a different style. While the Madia women like white colour the Korku women like bright colours. The men folk in the Madia Gonds like black colour particularly of the cap and if possible of the shirt also. In the Banjaras women put on bright coloured ghagara and their blouses leave the back almost uncovered. Their dress is profusely embroidered and studded with the pieces of mirror glass. The Kolam men put on rough dhoti and put on a bandi in place of a shirt. It is observed that during the last 20 to 25 years many tribals are adopting new costumes even in their rituals. For example, the Madia girls who dance at the time of the Dussera festival now carry bright coloured nylon or polyester sarees and blouses for putting on as an attire at the time of dancing as against the traditional Lugda which was the traditional dress for such occasions.

The religious chiefs, pujaris, bhagats, ghusadis have still maintained their traditional dresses to a large extent.

Fig. 2.1

Apart from the costumes and attire, flower garlands, necklaces of beads and malas are profusely put on by the dancers while dancing. All this gives it a typical glamour and the impression created helps to impress the onlookers. In some tribes the ornaments are so profuse that they simulate or take the place of costume. For example crowding of necklaces and malas cover the breast of women, and is playing the role of a blouse which they don't use. A typical characteristics of most tribals is the attraction towards those colours which they see in nature, *e.g.* white, black, green, red, blue and yellow.

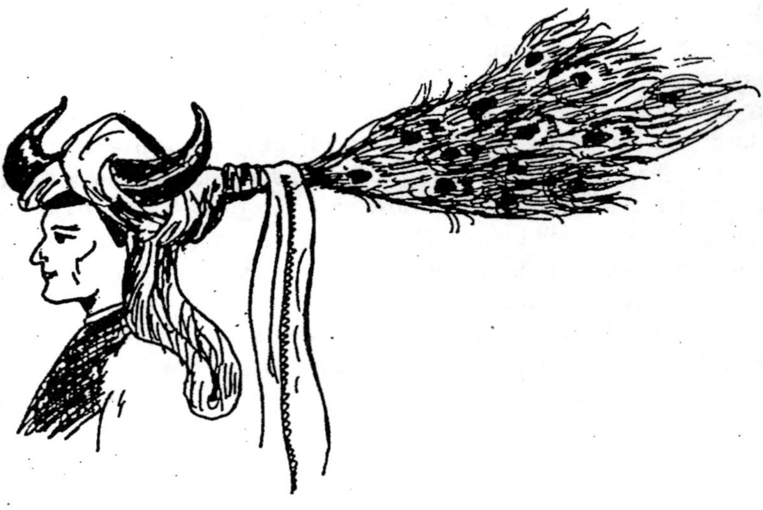

Fig. 2.2

Ornaments

The tribals are fond of ornaments. Specially, the women decorate their bodies with different ornaments spread over from the head to the feet. Most of the ornaments are made of brass, silver beads, stones or glass-beads. To these permanent ornaments are added flowers and coloured fruits or seeds of the trees. Though the general scheme of the ornament is similar, the forms and names differ from tribe to tribe.

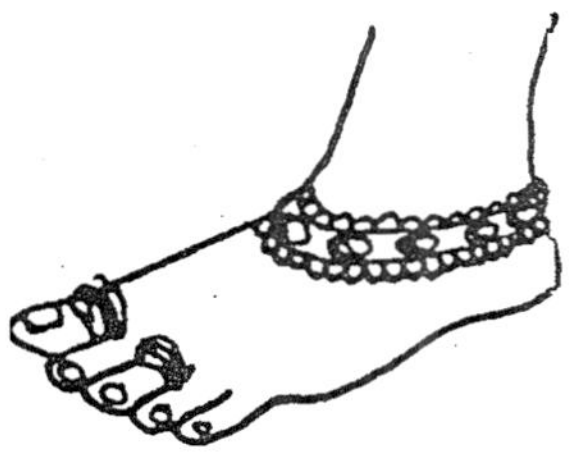

Fig. 2.3

Starting with the head we come across the *Bindi*, usually made of silver, and put on the head hanging upon the centre of the forehead. Silver chains are tied with the loops of hair and kept suspended across the head over the ears.

Fig. 2.4

The ears are also studded with various ornaments. The most common being the earrings made of silver or German-silver and also small silver-flowers on the upper pinna of the ear. Even big rings with beads are seen fixed on the upper pinna, while the ear-rings are kept suspended from the lower-lobes.

Nose rings and small flowers made of silver are also worn on the nose which is pierced for this purpose. At times a silver chain attached to the nose ring extends upto the ear and may be connected with the earrings.

Necklaces and Necklets of various types are very common. These are made of silver, brass, wooden-beads, colour stones, glass-beads or dry colour fruits etc. They are woven either in silver in threads or cotton threads or fibres from the trees. The forms and designs vary profusely. A typical ornament in the Gonds and particularly in the Madia-Gonds is a garland of old silver coins woven in black thick cotton string and suspended from the neck. This is called 'Zulki' or 'Zulkdabi'. Even thick silver rings are also put around the neck. In many tribes the open breasts of the women may be mostly covered by these necklaces and garlands put around the neck.

Fig. 2.5

On the upper arm, bracelets and rings of silver are put on by women and rarely by men, specially during dances. On the lower area, near the wrist, bangles of glass, rings of silver and brass are very common.

Fig. 2.6

Waist-belts (*Kamar pattas*) of silver are also worn by ladies of all ages. These are made of silver and have decorations carved on them, or studded with beads, or bells made of silver.

Fig. 2.7

On feet silver anklets jingling with pendant bells or beads are very common. On the toes and in the fingers toe-rings and other rings in the middle and index fingers are commonly worn. These may be of silver or brass.

Fig. 2.8

In addition to these ornaments garlands of flowers may be put around the neck or around the upper arm and the wrists. Even the men folk put on ornaments in which silver rings around the upper arm or rings in the ears or on the upper pinna of the ear are very common.

During dancing all these ornaments are meticulously used by the women and the men which imparts a special glamour to the show.

Apart from the musical bells (*Ghungroos*) which also serves as a decoration during the dance, the tinkling sound of these ornaments adds to the music.

In certain tribes, *e.g.* the Madia-Gonds small combs having teeth on both sides (*Phani*) are also put on the backside of the hair by the girls who are unmarried. Mostly these combs are given to the girls by their lovers as a token of love, hence sporting them on the hair is a matter of pride for the girl.

Tattooing

One of the decorations is the profuse tattooing on the body. It may be on the forehead, cheek, upper and forearms, upper leg (from the backside extending to the lower leg), on the hindside of the palm and the wrists. Different designs of flowers, trees, peacocks, triangles and rectangles, animals, Gods and Goddesses etc. are shown in the tattoos.

Tattooing is almost a part of the attire for the dancers. The tattooed body parts give a typical display in the light of the fire around which they dance to the tune of music.

Masks

In tribal dances masks are often used and are very popular. They have not only religious and ceremonial but even aesthetic importance in their dances. Certain ritual and social occasions require particular mask relevant to the theme while in some dances they are just meant for fun-making or frolicking.

It is difficult to define a mask but it may be defined as a form of disguise, an object frequently worn over or in front of the face to hide the identity of a person and by its own features to establish another being[1].

These masks are prepared by the tribals themselves and the technique is inherited traditionally. Roughly they can be classified as wooden masks, clay masks, bamboo masks, paper pulp masks. They are usually carved out with iron chisel and are prepared from soft wood like that of the Pangara tree or may be from teak wood which is rare. The mask should be light in weight.

The clay masks are prepared from fine clay soaked in water in which sticky juice or gum from the crust bark of the Mahua tree or the resins from the raw fruit of Bel tree are mixed. Cowdung may also be added to it so as to make it light. Then a mould is given to this mixture and dried in the sun. Later, typical features are carved on it and a glossy finish is given by using the resins or juice from different trees.

Fig. 2.9

Bamboo is ample in forest and mask may be prepared by weaving the fine threads of bamboo and giving different shapes on its surface. Clay and other colours may be added or bright coloured paper may be parted showing various features. Specially for showing the epic, kings, etc. the crown of the king and such other things this method is used. Triangular frames are often used for such things. Clay or wooden masks may be fixed on bamboo frames and thus different forms are created.

Fig. 2.10

Of late, many tribal communities have learned the art of making paper masks or paper pulp masks. For this purpose wet mud is given moulds and soaked. Newspaper sheets are pasted on it by using latex or resin from different trees. At times old newspapers or other papers are soaked in water for ten to fifteen days along with seeds of *Methi* (Fenugreek). Afterwards the two are finely ground into pulp and that paste is spread over mask moulds made of wet mud. It is dried for some days and the paper mask is lifted off from the mud mould. These masks are then painted with bright colours like black, white, yellow, green, blue, etc. which are mostly prepared from trees, flowers or coloured soil available in the area. However, these days they even bring colours from the market.

Fig. 2.11

Masks made from animal skin and hair may also be used. The faces of animals or the skin may be directly used or the skin may be moulded in particular manner to give it different appearances. Nose, eyes, ears etc. may be shown on it.

Fig. 2.12

In these different types of masks aperturers are left for eyes so that the wearer can see through it.

The tribals who use such masks include the Madia, the Korku, the Kolam, Pardhans, Bhils, Kokana, Khond, Pawra and many others. Especially when the epic stories from Ramayana and Mahabharata are played, Lord Ganesh, Hanuman, Krishna, Pandavas and particularly Ravana or Kumbhakarna are shown with masks. The other masks commonly used are of animals, like tigers, boar, bison, bear, deer, cow, buffalo, etc. The Madia Gonds use a rectangular shaped mask called Musada which has a low crown with a rectangular open mouth showing broad teeth and a hanging tongue. This is used during the ritual dance as a thanks giving service to God. The Kolam use masks during the gaon bandhani ritual and also while performing the dhemsa dances. The Madia Gonds also use the Bison horn head-gear which has two horns placed over triangular shaped woven basket put on as a headgear while dancing. Demons and Asuras are also shown with big eyes, large noses, wild open large mouth, big sharp teeth and hanging tongue. For frolicking one of the dancers in a group may carry a long bamboo or bamboo structure at the top of which a mask may be placed. In Dandar dances use of masks is very common. In the Korku tribals the 'Khamm' dance which is a ritual drama masks of Ganesh and other deities are used.

Fig. 2.13

Thus the masks represent an aesthetic sense and also fulfil the role playing required in the dances. They are mostly prepared in an indigenous manner from locally available materials and display the imaginativeness and artistic skills of the tribal population.

Fig. 2.14

Musical Instruments

The tribal people have evolved their own musical instruments and prepare them indigenously. Even in this sphere they are self-dependent and utilise all the natural products available in the forest. Roughly, these musical instruments may be classified in four classes, *viz*.

(i) Drum type instruments of percussion
(ii) Blow-wind instruments
(iii) Stringed instruments
(iv) Solid-stroke instruments, *e.g.* Cymbal

The Drum-type instruments include the *Dhol*, *Daf*, *Pāgai*, *Nagārā*, *Māndal*, etc.

The *Dhol* is very popular in tribal dances. Dhols may be of different sizes and types. Skin of a goat or deer is stretched and fitted on the two open sides of a hollow spherical piece carved from a log of teak or tamarind tree; or prepared from earthenware. The drums are beaten by wooden sticks. A big dhol may be kept on earth while a smaller one is suspended by strings from the drummers neck while beating, the sound resounds and is grave.

Dholki is a small dhol and is always suspended from neck and beaten by hands.

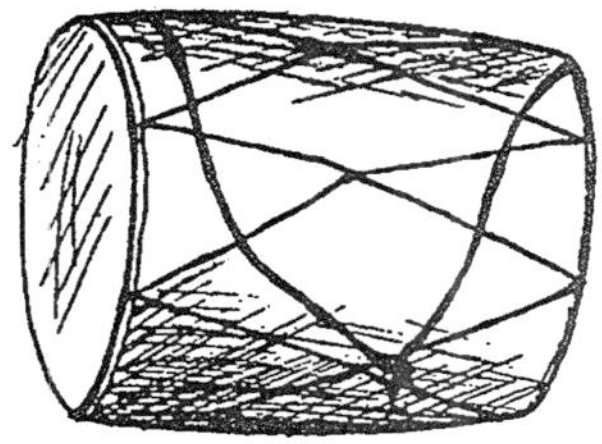

Fig. 2.15: Dhol

Pagai is also like dholki and simulates the *Mridangam* popular in southern Indian musical instruments.

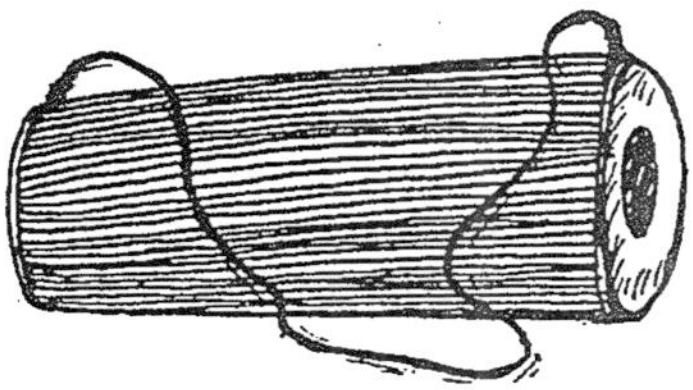

Fig. 2.16: Pagai

Nagara is a big bowl shaped drum with animal skin drawn over the mouth of the bowl. It is beaten by club-shaped sticks and the big humming sound spreads far away.

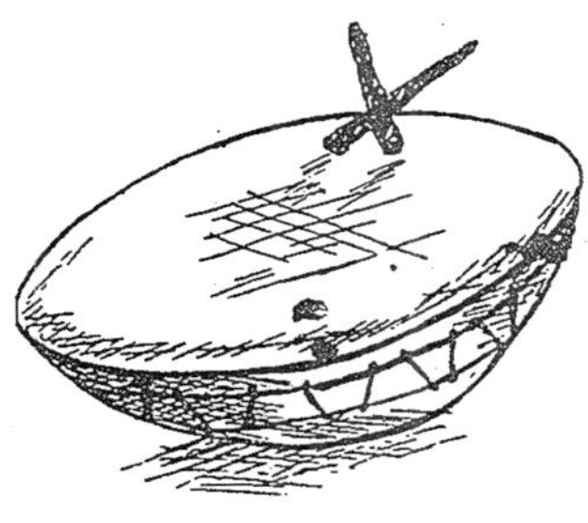

Fig. 2.17: Nagara

Daf is also prepared by stretching animal skin on one side of a big circular ring of wood. It is beaten by slim sticks. The ring is about six inches in breadth and 25-30 inches in diameter.

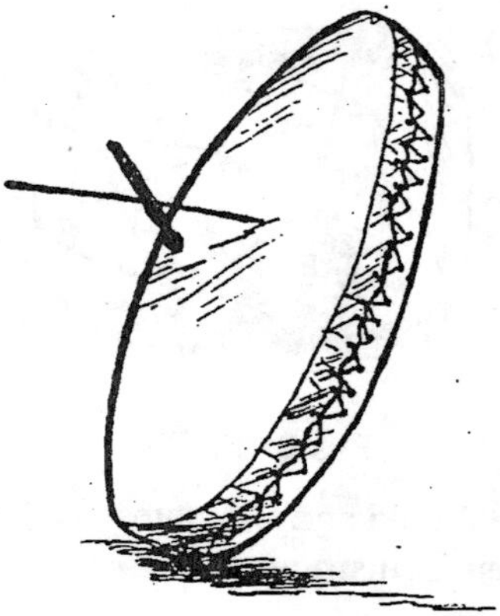

Fig. 2.18: Daf

Kundudi is small (about 10′′ – 12′′ in diameter) bowl-shaped instrument over which animal skin is stretched and is beaten by two small sticks. It is used by the person who directs the rhythm for the music and dance by slinging it from neck or ties on waist. This is very common in Madia-Gond dances. *Timki* is also similar in shape and use.

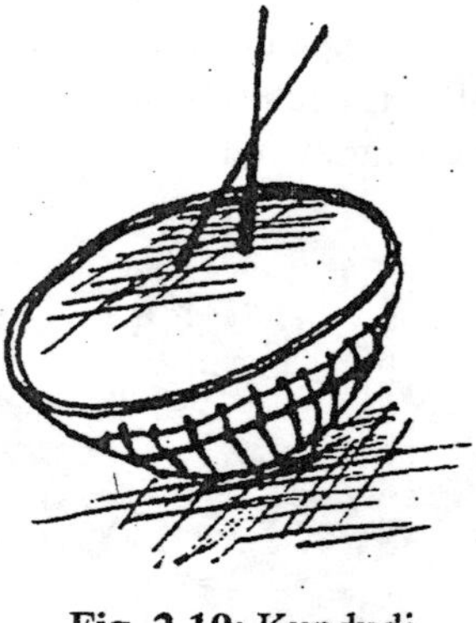

Fig. 2.19: Kundudi

Dhăk /Dăk is also a similar instrument prepared from the tender skin of animals, small in size and used at the time of annual death ritual, or when some one is in trance or on some pooja occasion.

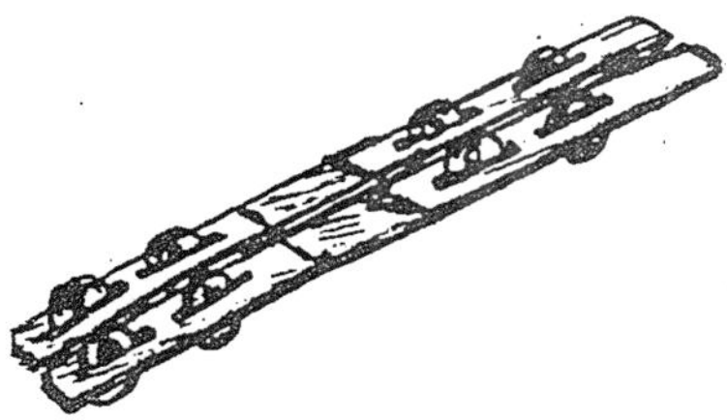

Fig. 2.20: Chitkora

The stretched skin on these instruments is warmed on fire so that the sound becomes clear and resonant.

Fig. 2.21: Tal

Wind Instruments

Wind is blown by mouth through these instruments producing sound and hence these may be better described as blow-wind instruments. Dried fruits like gourds, bamboo, wood, animal horns, etc. are used for preparing such instrument. Flute is a very common instrument in many tribals. Others are like trumpets.

Tutari, Tarpa, Pawri etc. come under the class.

Tutari is a trumpet prepared from the horns of animals.

Pawari is prepared from dry white gourd, which is selected depended upon its shape. Small pieces of bamboo are fitted for blowing air and holes are prepared on the bamboo piece for modulating the notes of music. The mouth piece may be of horn or toddy leaf.

Tarpa: The Warlis use this instrument and is prepared from dry white gourd of a particular shape. It simulates the *Pungi* of a snake-charmer. Two small bamboo pieces are fitted on one side of the gourd while on the other side of a blow-horn, prepared from Toddy leaf is fitted. The dancers dance around the tarpa-blower.

Piri, alternately called Biri is also a wind instrument made from horn of a deer, bamboo and white gourd. Its sound is full of melody.

Pava is like a big flute prepared from a bamboo, 2½ to 3 feet in length.

Stringed Instruments

These include the instruments in which metal strings or hair are used; like that in Violin, Sitar or Tanpura.

Ghangli: It looks like a Veena. It is very popular among Warli tribals.

Fig. 2.22: Ghangli

Two round-shaped dry pumpkins are used and fitted at the two ends of a bamboo stick. Two bent pegs are fitted at the two ends of the bamboo and metal wires are fitted on them. The player holds the two pumpkins in his arm-pit and plays on the wire strings to produce music. Ghangli is played at on festive and auspicious occasion or while worshipping the Goddess of harvest called Kansari. It is also used while celebrating child birth.

Kingri is an instrument of the Pardhans/Thotis. Kingri or Bana are similar. These are prepared by using a wooden head or dry pumpkin. On the side which is open thin animal skin is fitted by stretching and a bamboo is fitted on it like that in a violin. Hair of horse or other animal are tightly fitted. Metal wire strings are also used. A small wooden bow with hair strings is also prepared for playing on the *Bana*.

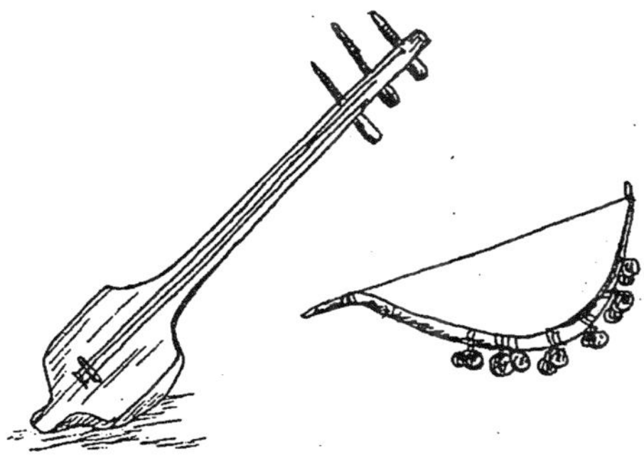

Fig. 2.23: Kingri

Bana is prepared on some Sunday in the Hindu month of *Vaishakh* which is supposed to be auspicious day. Fast is observed and a goat is sacrificed before a tree. On the next day wood is brought from that tree and Bana is prepared while singing songs in praise of Gods. Bana may be of a particular type when it is called a *Rajnengi Bana* which is a traditional musical instrument of Pardhans. Kingri may be of a particular type called Hirobai Kingri which is a traditional instrument of the Thotis. Both the tribes, *viz.* the *Pardhans* and *Thotis* are known as minstrels.

Tuntune: Skin is stretched over a hollow bowl on outer side and a metal wire or hair of horse is fitted over it. A bamboo stick is fitted. It is played either by thumb or by a hair-bow.

Dholki is often accompanied by Tuntune.

Dera: This is prepared from a big earthen circular pot. Toddy or Teak leaves are fitted on the mouth of the Dera, and sound is produced by long stick. Dera is first worshipped.

Kathya is an instrument prepared out of brass utensil. Animal skin is stretched over it. Long hairs are fitted as strings. Melodius sound comes out when played on the strings.

Solid-Stroke Instruments

These simulate the cymbal or the lezim. The sound is produced due to the stroke of a solid wooden instrument fitted with small metal-plates.

Chitkora: This simulates a lezim as well as a cymbal and is made up of about 2 feet long pieces of wood, two or three metal plates are fitted on these pieces of wood leaving a distance of 4 to 5 inches. This is always in a pair and place is left at the centre for the grip of palm. Both the pieces are held in one hand and made to strike on each other. It creates a typical metallic sound.

Tal: This is similar to the above one but a smaller one – about 6 to 7 inches in length. It is very popular for singing religious songs popularly known as Bhajanas.

Bhangsar: It is a typical instrument used by tribals in the Western Ghats in Maharashtra. In a big brass-utensil a tender stick of the *saradi* legume, is made to stand erect by using wax. Then water is poured in the utensil and the thumb and the pointing fingers are rubbed on the stick in the utensil to produce sound.

Ghungroo: These are musical bells producing musical sound. Bells of different sizes are used while dancing. Small belts on which small musical bells are fitted are put on around the waist or on feet ankles etc. While dancing, fine jerks are given to these *ghungroos* producing rhythm as well as melodious sound. The Bada Madia Tribals from Gadchiroli district use these *ghungroos* profusely in their Rela s s dances.

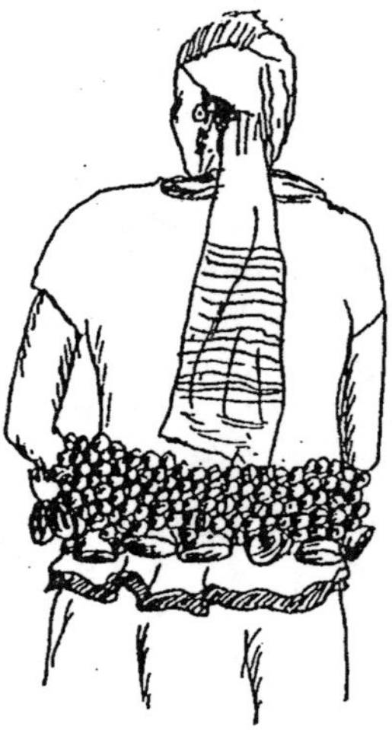

Fig. 2.24

Fig. 2.25: Ghungroos (Musical Bells)

After studying these different types of instruments of the tribals one feels that they were the original forms from which many of our modern musical instruments must have developed. Similarly all these instruments are locally prepared from whatever is available in their areas. The workmanship is also very fine and various designs are carved or painted on instruments. Every tribal knows the instruments used in his area and they learn to play on them right from their childhood. Though most of the instruments are commonly seen, some are typical to certain areas or tribes.

	Tribe	*Area*	*Instrument*
1.	Madia Gond	Gadchiroli distt.	Dhol
	-do-	-do-	Pagai
	-do-	-do-	Ghungroo
	-do-	-do-	Kundudi
	-do-	-do-	Chitkora
2.	Pardhan, Thoti	Yavatmal distt.	Bana
	-do-	-do-	Kingri, Daf
3.	Warli	Thane distt.	Tarpa, Ghangli
4.	Bhil	Dhule distt.	Biri
	-do-	-do-	Flute
5.	Korku	Amravati distt.	Flute, Tiprya
	-do-	-do-	Tutari
6.	Kolam	Yavatmal distt. Chandrapur distt.	Daf
	-do-	-do-	Tasha
	-do-	-do-	Tutari

Classification of Tribal Dances

Based on the study of tribal dances broad generalisations have been attempted to show certain common characteristics of folk-dances. These are:

(i) *Simplicity*: The movements of body and limbs are simple and can be performed by any member from their community, and simulate physical exercises; movements of animals etc.

(ii) *The Style* of the song and the rhythm are simple. The music is also simple, and in many cases a four-note music, *viz. Sā, Sā, Ni, Pa*. Hence community participation is facilitated.

(iii) The dances are traditional and the whole community participates. Dances are not influenced by any individual or a choreographer but are conceived and performed by the whole community.

(iv) Use of masks, make-up of the body and face and use of feathers, bones, flowers, leaves, animal skins and horns or decorative articles prepared out of these like garlands of beads, flowers, etc. are common in all tribal dances; variations depending upon their natural environment.

In a tribal community there are no spectators but all are performers, persons of all ages joining the dances. Tribal dances may be classified taking different criteria as bases.

Based on *participation* the dances may be classified as:

(i) Women's dances
(ii) Men's dances
(iii) Mixed dances

Depending upon the *occasion* these may be classified as:

(i) Religious or Ritual dances
(ii) Festival dances
(iii) Social dances

Depending upon *performing style* they may be classified as:

(i) Dancing in circles — by repeating the round and stepping two steps forward and one step backward while the dancers look back — is a typical style of many primitive tribes. They either join hands or stretch one arm around the shoulders of the partner thus forming a ring of dancers;

(ii) In another form they form a semi-circle and zoom ahead to the tune and rhythm of music like a tidal wave, then again slide back a little, and then surging ahead with a gusto;

(iii) The third form simulates a procession; and

(iv) The fourth form is of music backed physical exercises simulating acrobatics or the modern aerobics.

REFERENCE

1. Tribhuwan, D. Robin, Jose, Jaya, "Commercialisation of Tribal Masks – An Imperative Need", *Tribal Research Bulletin,* Vol XVIII, No. 1, March, 1996, Pune.

3

Folk Dance – Songs of Tribals

MARRIAGE

Marriage is a festive occasion for the whole of the village. Clan exogamy and tribe endogamy is observed. Usually marriages are settled by the boys and girls themselves, however, the elders put a mark of approval by deciding upon the bride-price and such other terms as may be found necessary. The marriage ceremony is performed at the bridegroom's place and as such the bride's party goes to the groom's place. The bride-price is paid partly in cash and partly in kind like paddy, goat, pair of bullocks etc. as per the terms. In some tribes a groom who is unable to pay the bride-price has to work at the place of the would-be father-in-law for a fixed term which is settled by elders. He is called *Ghar-jawai* or *Dhaglya* etc.

Marriage is performed in a pandal erected at groom's place. Depending upon the traditions of the tribe, the pillars from the tree-trunks of particular trees are necessary and even their number is fixed. But the main pillar-around which the ritual is performed is in many tribes of the *Salai* (*Basvellia serrata*) tree.

Use of turmeric powder is common which is applied to the body of the bride and of the groom. Bathing and pouring of water on the couple, or touching of the left toe of the bride by the right toe of the groom, wading through the heap of cowdung are some of the typical rituals which symbolise the performance of the marriage. Of late, due to introjection, some tribals have adopted the methods of rice-throwing, and singing of five or eight auspicious stanzas

(*Mangalashtaka*) at the time of marriage. But this is an adoption from the traditional Hindu culture.

Feast is an important part of the marriage festival. This is followed by drinking of liquor – mostly *Mahua* – which is specially brewed for the occasion. At times, while settling the marriage itself, the quantity of liquor (*e.g.* 7 or 8 *Gunds* – Barrels of brass) is promised to be served at the function. This is followed by dances which are performed by all and both parties join. Women of all ages join these dances. Usually, while dancing, men beat drums and play on instruments, while women sing in a chorus. Bon-fires are made and they dance throughout the night in its light.

The songs sung at various stages in the marriage rituals include various themes, like amorous love and affection towards the bride, bride-price, teasing the men and women and even the bridegroom, sentiments on the separation of the bride from her parents and family, and love between the bride and the groom etc.

Here it is attempted to present songs sung on various occasions during a marriage ceremony in different tribes. The readers will realise that the sentiments and feelings expressed are not only similar to each other but are similar to those which we entertain in our modern culture.

Gondi Marriage Songs

Before, during and after the marriage ceremony different songs are sung while dancing. A few are cited below:-

Song sung at the time of engagement

Rela s s Relaa s s s Rerela s s s
Batal Kitibal Rajale Satyer Raja Vani
Nime Uti Julajula Aal Seke
Nag Bari Kisi Baba
Nana Siyale Sile Beti
Nana Aval Sita
Babona Kortal Pedki Tindavata
Joda Joda Aavana Korate

Meaning

The bride expresses her feelings on separation from her parents. She asks the bridegroom, as to when will she meet her warm loving father, and her mother Sita? When will she be able to return to her parents and take meals with her parents?

A Welcome Song

For welcoming the guests at the marriage *pandal* this song is sung.

Rela s Re s Rela s s s
Udme Makun Chadar Wata
Makun Udle Khurching Wata
Khurching Aaune Pure Maike Mandana
Aakashi Mandap, Dhartari Mandate Wata

Meaning

For our guests spread a bedsheet (Chadar), for sitting our guests bring chairs (Khurchi), the sky (Aakashi) is the roof and the earth (Dhartari) is the base (for sitting).

Marriage Songs of the Madia-Gonds

A Welcome Song

A song to welcome the guests at the marriage *pandal* is given below:

Yere vāiro, yere vāiro
Marmit vāiro, marmit vāiro, Re Rela s s s s
Marmit vāi, kabad kisi antu
Nimmā sangon, nannā sangon, jivaasta vāi
Sangona diwānā barivāyo, Re Rela s s s s
Re s s Rela a .. s s s s

Meaning

Welcome guests, welcome. Don't break promise, do come.
We are yours, you are ours—our precious guests.

Let us join to celebrate with jubilation and enjoy ourselves.

Here is a song sung in the marriage dance which depicts the physical union between a boy and a girl, and also indicates the sexual freedom which is given before marriage, and amorous love.

Re la, Re Ree la
Kormulateke omu ró éh dada dada
Korung korung kimu Ró éh dada dada... 1
Marka maratgā omu Ró éh dādā dādā
Makāng markāng Kimu Ro éh dada dada... 2
Ivur pekur undi pegutun ontur Ró éh—dādā dādā
Dodāng dodāng omu Ró éh dādā dādā
Dodang dodang kimu Ró éh dādā dādā... 3

Meaning

Oh *Dādā* (here, 'friend') take her to the corner where the hens are kept; and do as the hen and cock do.
Oh Dādā take her with you below the mango tree; Oh! see she has been taken there and (he) is doing something. (These) two boys have taken her on the banks of a stream, Oh! Dādā, (she) has been taken by two boys to the stream; and (they) have done something.

A few songs used for marriage 'Relas' are given below. The girls are teasing the bridegroom.

Song indicating bride-price

Rela Re Rela s s s s
Jodi jodi indādi
Vanji vālvāl dādi, Vanji vāl vāl...
Gādā nukā doste Dādi, vanji vāl vāl...
Aske nivā jodi Dādi, vanji vāl vāl...
Punam jodi dorko Dadi, vanji val val...
Korat pāri loney Dādi, vanji vāl vāl...
Durat bokdā dohanéké,
Aske nivā jodi, dorko Dādi,
Vanji vāl vāl Dādi, vanji vāl vāl...

Meaning

> Sing all in pairs, sing in pairs (and tell the bridegroom) Oh, Dadi (bridegroom), when you will give one cart-load of paddy then only you will get the bride. Oh, Dadi, you must pay the price if you want to take away the nice bride. Hence you give paddy first. Dadi, you give a goat, then only you can take away the bride, you cannot take her away till you pay the bride-price.

Send-off to the bride

Another song is addressed to the bride. This is a send-off to the bride.

Rela s s Re-reela s s s
Sāli metā hanum dādi
Kinir, vinir hanum dādi, Re—Relo s s
Nivā dāyanā jodi dādi,
Kinir, vineer hanum dadi
Kinir, vinir, kinir, vinir, Re-Reelo s s.

Meaning

> Oh, bride (Dādi) your husband is taking you with him for a year. So, you go with him smiling and dancing. He is now your life-partner, so go with him smiling and dancing.

In Madia-Gond marriages, the marriage ritual is performed around a central pillar called *Mund* which is a thick stump of the *Salai* (*Boswellia serrata*) tree which is an auspicious tree. They believe that Lord Persapen's abode is on the *Salai* tree. A marriage song sung at the time of marriage in the pandal very aptly, tries to reflect the feelings of the bride's party on the *Salai mund* and is an example of transferred epithet.

Ree s s Reelo, Ree s s Re s s Lo s
Sale Munda Royta
Niva Mulu Royta
Neva Relo Muluye, Ree s s Reelo s s
Pata Hoteke Natoske
Niva Relo Muluye, Ree s s Reelo s s

Dharmam Pata Osta
Sale Munda Royta
Niva Relo Muluye, Ree s s Reelo s s
Niku Pohchi Daynu
Niva Jiva Oointa
Niva Relo Muluye, Ree s s Reelo s s

Meaning

The pillar (*Mund*) of *Salai* has bent, similarly, your relatives (bride's party) have also bent (due to the mental burden of separation of bride from them after marriage).

Your younger sister and all relatives have bent.

All of them are unnecessarily singing song which is not a real expression of their happiness (That means though they are feeling the pangs of separation they are putting on the show of gaiety by singing songs). The *Salai* pillar has bent.

Now (after marriage) all your people will return back home, leaving you (the bride) along with the bridegroom, and your heart will shrink due to the pangs of separation from your relatives. Your sister and relatives are worthlessly singing the songs.

The feelings expressed in this song are poignant and universal, and the metaphorical way of charging the epithets on the *Mund* are indicative of the natural literary instinct of these illiterate primitive tribals.

Pardhan Marriage Songs*

These are songs enquiring about the clan and family of the groom and bride.

Jaatee ro baatee riyore dada?
Jaatee ro baatee bhidee ro dada?
Chandekar, Bhondekar, neet navral
kummekar jaatire na riyore dada.

---

* Some of the songs are taken from Dr. S.R. Murkute's Book: *Socio-cultural study of Scheduled Tribe: The Pardhans of Maharashtra*; (1991), Concept Pub. Co., New Delhi.

Meaning

Oh, dada, to which class (clan) do you belong?
I am from a responsible family from Chanda (Chandrapur), I am not a scoundrel.

The Bride

Yer dehaakee lata de
Jaatee re baatee miyaale sango
Yer dahaakee lata de
Jaatee* dheke miyale sango.

Meaning

Who is this beautiful girl and to which Gotra (*Clan*) does she belong?
She is engrossed in taking bath. She belongs to a particular clan.

Turmeric Songs

While grinding and applying turmeric powder to be bride and groom these songs are sung.

Baad laadeenaa rotaa O
Naavonee yaayaa O
Laadeenaa rotaa O,
Naavonee yaayaa O
Jaataa Maalonee araataa O,
Naavonee yaayaa O
Kaishaar Zuraanee araataa O,
Naavonee yaayaa O
Ladeena rotaa O,
Naavonee yaayaa O
Zaaraanaa zuraanee araataa O,
Naavonee yaayaa O.

---

* Here they add the name.

Meaning

This song is sung by the women while grinding turmeric. They say, we are most unhappy. Who are the relatives of that beautiful girl?

Those people are also unhappy. All the things and people are unhappy because they will be parting company with the beautiful girl.

Pichee noraa levaalaa vo aange vo
Pichee noraa levaalaa vo
nee maanataa sireeyaale aange vo
daadaana maanta vaayaa vo
daamo jode kisee aange vo
niva sireeyaal tatee vo
niva maantaa sireeyaal aange
daadaanaa maantaa vaayo vo.

Meaning

Come, one and all for grinding turmeric. Here is your dear sister. But she is not liked by my brother.

You spent money for finding her, but my brother does not like her. Tears are coming out from your eyes while grinding turmeric but, he will not care for you.

Daadaa re daadaa indaale bovo
Dore to daadaane mutaale bovo
Pahilo to pichee naatendor melyaane
Doosaar,pichee naaten dor Bheemaane.

Meaning

Whom will this sister call?
First she will call the chief of the village. Then she will call the God and offer turmeric to him.
Then she will call Bhimdeo and all other Gods from the village.
After applying turmeric, the groom is bathing. This song is sung at that time.

Aaatee kaakaanaa siree baasingaa,
Koeekaa raajaaka betaa angorikaa baithe vo,
Raajaaka betaa angorika baithe va,
Dai – daadan siree baasingaa.

Meaning

His (groom) life depended upon his uncle, aunt and brother. Now his days have come. He is the prince of the occasion, taking bath here.

This song is sung while erecting the Mandav (*Pandal*).

Hono kaa kona, bhaaee re mevaa,
Maandav to uthaavo.
Chaarojee bhaai meraa,
Maandav to uthaavo.
Saaleka deree re deree,
Jamun ka saayaa,
Chaandee ka adaavaa,
Sone kee adulee,
Bhaale to bhaale, bhaai re mera,
Maandav to uthaavo.

Meaning

Let us all cooperate for erecting this pandal. We wish that this pandal should be a good one. The pillars are of Salai and Jamun trees and the canopy is of silver and gold. This will be decorative for the pandal.

Bride-price (Kharcha)

There is a custom of sending bride-price (*Kharcha*) from the groom's side to the bride's side. On the second day of marriage while reaching the '*Kharcha – Saman*' to the marriage pandal at bride's place this song is sung.

Kumbhaareen baaee vo kumbhaar kuthe gela,
Haatee kudaree dharalaa baaee,
Maatee khandaalaa gelaa.

Maatee khaandataa khaandataa baaee,
Paay modoon gelaa. ...1
Haatee sota dharla baaee,
Gadhe raakhaale gelaa,
Gadhe raakhataa raakhataa baaee,
Haat modoon gelaa. 2

Meaning

Where has the Kumbhar gone? On that occasion the Kumbhar (earthen potmaker) went with a sickle to dig the soil and O'baaee he got his leg broken while digging soil.
He went with a stick to keep the herd of donkeys but O baaee while keeping the donkies he got his hand broken.

Many Marathi words are used in this song which shows the influence of Marathi language on the Pardhans.

Another Kharcha Song

Hai kharchaa jaate hai,
Hai kharchaa jaate
Navarde vaachyaa maandavee navardevaachya maandavee
Hai kharchaa jaate hai,
Hai kharchaa jaate ...1
Konaachyaa maandavee, konaachyaa maandavee
Aaagaashee maandavee,
Aaagaashee maandavee,
Dharatee re boholaa, dharatee re boholaa
Hai kharchaa hai, hai kharchaa jaate hai ...2

Meaning

This song also is in the context of *Kharcha* and is sung while carrying the kharcha (*Bride-price*).

To whose pandal is this *Kharcha* going?
The kharcha is going to the pandal of the bridegroom
This pandal has got the roof of the sky and the earth is the altar

where the marriage is performed.
The metaphors used are remarkable.

The newly married bride and groom are seated on a carpet and couples from the town assemble. The oldest couple starts bathing the newly married couple by pouring water and others follow. This song is sung on that occasion.

Jati ro baati reeyona saamiyaa pati lataa de
Hai laadee samee patee lataa de
(Dhekyaa) reeyonaa ladee saameeyaa hulaale vaayenee de
Saameeyaa patan neti ladaa, naavorbaaboo rangaanoor
Hai ladaa naavor baaboo rangaanoor
Nivor baaboo rangaan notee, jodaa chaading waatika de
Hai laadee saameeyaa halaale vaayenee de
Saameeyaa hulaale baayaan netee navaa aavatee rangaal ro
Hai saameeyaa pattee tataa de
Hai laadee saapeeyaa hulaale vaalaa de
Oreete udaan netee duleraa naavor tammoo rangaanoor
Niror tammoo rangaan netee, kodaa singaroo taatika de
Hai laadee pichee sokaale vaalaa de
Pichee sokaan netee duleraa navaa taange rangaal de
Nivaa taange rangaan netee, saree khaagoraa sikaan de
Hai laadee yere toreele vaalaa de
Yer toraan netee duleraa navaa selaal rangaal ro
Selaal rangaan netee, cholee dikalee taattikaa de
Hai laadee dhotee siyaale vaalaa de
Karayaale noote pandaree noole laadee
Agene riyonaa raahutee de
Hai laadee raahutee hulaale vaayenee de
Raahutee hulaan netee duleraa, inhaakyaa dhekyaa hulaanvorro
Inhaakya dhekyaa hulaan netee
Gonaa gaamding vaatika de
Hai laadee saameeyaa patee lataa de.

Meaning

Whose youthfulness is burning? O dear Devi, come and see.
"O my dear lover, my father will be angry".

"I shall spread a carpet on the path of your father and shall welcome him. But you do come."
"O my dear my mother will be angry how can I come?"
"O my beloved don't worry, I shall send a horse-driven cart for your mother but you do come."
"My brother will be angry and shall scold me when I come."
"O dear, don't worry I shall send a horse for your brother and make him happy."
"My brother's wife will scold me."
"I shall give her ornaments and saree. She will be pleased. My sister will block your way but you don't worry I shall give her a saree and blouse. Don't worry about the children in our town. I shall give them woollen blankets but you do come."

Such dialogues continue in the song while dancing on the rhythm of drums.

Advice to the Bridegroom on His Clan and Origin

Jaatee vo baatee miyaanee yaayaa
Jaatee vo miyaanee yaayaa
Aavo nivaate selomee vehaavo
Baalo vehaa burote vehaa
Baalo vehaa burote vehaa
Vaattaal kaatyaatoon haale dhaadaamee
Pahaanaa kaatyaatoon haate sedomee
Nivaa sedomee vehaaoor
Bhaalo te vehaa buro te vehaa
Baateenee sedomee
Vehkaar kuvaaraa?
Sedomee muchchook jaalamma vo yaayaa
Jaayaate vanjeer khand naave yaayaanee
Paaloke tallate yetaaka vo yaayaa
Nivaa sedomee vehaavaa
Aaagas aandoor baabaa ro kuvaara
Dhaartoree aande aavaal ro
Dhaar teree zele kitaaro kuvaara
Niva sedomee kenjaaro.

Meaning

O mother, tell me which type of milk have I drunk? You please tell me either this way or that way.
Please tell me how I came to this world from which clan my blood has come?
Why are you silent? Tell me quickly or else I shall have to cut your tongue.
O my dear child what shall I tell you?
The sky which is the father of this universe, is your father.
This earth which is the mother of everyone, is your mother.
This earth has reared you up.
This is the secret of your birth, clan and caste.

A Patadi (religious singer) Tells the Groom about his Origin

Re re naa re re naa baabo re s s
Hore kaa bore bhee baabo re
Re re naa re re naa baabo re
Hore ka bhekere baabo re
Nivaate koraataa kuvaaraanaa baabo re
Remeete niltonaa Javaneete vaatonaa
Keyaate mivore paataaleen baabo re
Daadaanaa udeekaane kutoode
Paataalee udaaneer bi laate
Bhideere chavdinge taaraanoor paataadee
Taayee aanaa baabolaa pundeeka
Saateeke maan donge Raamgaade
Penuke mandamunge Jaamgaade
Jango lingo Hirajyotee sedonee
Jaai eme kunvaaranaa pundeekee
Ree naa re re naa baa bo re
Hore kaa bore bhee baabo re.

Meaning

Who is my father? My father is rich.
O babaa (father), I am your fond-son.
O dreamer of the happy future for me, O babaa tell me

information about our clan.
I come up under the umbrella of your affection.
I have become a youth of which you are aware.
Call the (Patadi) religious priest. I shall sit before him. He will take out the religious book and give me information about my origin.
The religious priest (Patadi) tells,
"At Ramgadh there is a temple of seven *satis*. At Jamgadh the Gods worshipped in your clan are present. Jango, Lingo and Hirojyoti are the main Gods of your clan. This is the secret of your clan. Are you satisfied?"

Advice to the Bride

Re re naa, re renaa naare don
Bore aandoor naave badoor don
Siree to bhaghavaane nave kuvaaree oner don
Dharteree aavaale naave kavaareenaa don
Bore to aandure naave bainore pepee
Raajaa kaa kaaroonaale bainore pepee
Injee koone saaraa kaare don naave sone ka baabolaa
Aaana handaakaane raapo re sukaare ka haabolaa
Rande diyaana aana pohaanenaa baabolaa
Dusrona rota re singare aana baabolaa
Rone ka haakare sindee re baabolaa
Rachaavaale hokaare sindaane baabolaa
Re re naa re naave baabolaa

This song gives advice to the bride who is going to her-in-law's place.

Meaning

The bride's father says the father of my dear daughter is the God himself, and the mother is the mother earth. King Karma is her uncle. O dear daughter you are lucky.
The daughter says – "Because there is famine (poverty) on our side am I lucky?
If I go to my father-in-law's place shall I prosper?

Why are you bored of me so early? I am like a guest. I am some one else's property since my birth.
When you needed something you used to call me very often. O baba, when I go. Whom will you call?"

After the hair of the groom are cut the groom's sisters collect the hair in the pouch of their sarees and sing this song.

Daadee angaale vale baai behonaa lee
Nivaa daadeekaa aangeekaa daadaa
Baatee daayaayo siki ro
Mula daayojo sika naave behonaa
Lamee dayejo sikaa vo
Daadee anjee levaslaa baaee behonaa
Dhokee miyale indaanukaa daadaa
Mhaskee miyaale indarooke ro
Daadee anjeele vaayonaa daadaa
Baatee dayeejee sikee ro
Matya khagora sika baaee baahonaa
Daadee anjeele vaalaa ho
Sonaar miyaale indaa umhe daadaa
Kaasaar miyaale do vahe so
Daadee anjeele vaayonaa daạdaa
Baatee daayeejee sikareen ro
Nivaa rone vedaabaai bechonaa
Nivaa saagure vehaa kaho
Sarag hattaa keretaa hane
Taane legaataa khaprel ro
Had nivaa bohonaanaa rone
Naake akhidaange sikee ro.

Meaning

The groom. "Come to collect my hair".
Sister - "What will you give me?"

The groom "I shall give you a cow, I shall give you a buffalo but you come without fail".

Sister, "If you give me a cow people will call daughter of a cow-herd keeper. If you give me a buffalo they will call me daughter of a buffalo keeper, I don't want this, what will you give?"

Groom, "I shall give you a golden bangle and copper ornaments".

Sister, "Then people will call me a goldsmith's daughter or a coppersmith's daughter. I don't want these what will you give?"

Groom, "Give me your home address, I shall come to your home to invite you".

Sister, "My tiled house is in the midst of tall trees. You come there. You always remember me and that will be my gift."

Song Sung while Welcoming the Groom

Jaatee ro baatee riyyonaa
Mundaa vayaa lata
Mahore naalenjaa maahonaa
Nahore maalenjaa naahonaa
Riyonaa laadee de
Mundaa vayaa lata
Daadaonaa Jodeeto
Riyyor aakhaadaa dehakee laatore
Shindaare maan tulaa dore
Riyoor aakhaadaa dehakee lantore
Markaa Foreeng kaankanor
Riyyor aakhaadaa dehakee laatore

Meaning

Who are these people?
They are coming in a procession.
Are they from the bridegroom's side?
The Sun God and the Moon God are protecting them.
Who is that brave boy?
He is playing very well.
This youth with a big head, beautiful eyes, stout arms and an impressive chest is playing very well.

This song is sung while a *Kumkum tilak* is put on the forehead of the bride.

Kahekaa chauk likhiyo baabolaa?

Gulyaada chaukaa likhiyo kaniyaa
Kaahekaa chauk likhiyo baabolaa?
Kamkaataa chaukaa likhiyo baabolaa
Chauk udaalevaalaa ho kaniyaa.

Meaning

All of you who have come for this ceremony will please apply *chouk* to the bride.

The bride says I don't want Gulal, Turmeric powder. The names of items like Flour, Munjamoti, Gajmoti, etc. are added and song is continued. For a bride *Kumkum tilak* is most precious. So she says—

Kukootaa chauke udaa betee sukho
Kukoonge kukoonge dislikaa re
Julavee julavaa kaasonekaa do
Khaagoraa sakaree bee karone kaare
Bade chauke udore kaa do
Anaa chouke udore re

Meaning

The bride says, "I want and would like Kumkum. I don't want ornaments. I don't want chain or Khagora (an ornament). I don't want anything. O'Baba I had never demanded these things."

When the priest announces the marriage those present throw rice (*Akshada*) on the couple. The following song of five stanzas is sung which is a pious song:

Tarhar Kanyadan

Maa do vedoor laadee
Saavaatee udnul de
Tarhaar kanyaadaan ...1
Mee do vaandoor laadee
Dhaadmiteene udnoor de
Ganjaa ghote kundoor de
Tarhaar kanyaadaan ... 2
Mee daunaa naalee de laadee

Ulleenaa ganjee de maa
Daunaa maalee de laadee
Sonotaange kamadee
Tarhaar kanyaadaan ...3
Mee do paisaa lobhee
Nikum hare maatur de
Nivood nelee udmoor de
Tarhaar kanyaadaan ... 4
Suno Narmadaa, suno re Gangaa
Suno naagareeke lok de
Nivaa kaayaa naavaa kaay de
Tarhaar kanyaadaan ... 5

Meaning

My father always sat in the shadow; let this marriage prove auspicious.

Your father always sat in bright sunshine preparing Ganja, let this marriage be auspicious.

Your father has put a chain of onions around his neck, my father puts on a golden chain, let this marriage prove auspicious.

Your father is greedy of money and hence he has lost you. He is smoking Ganja and is sitting below the *Hivra* tree. Let this marriage prove auspicious.

O, Narmada, Ganga, listen, O, the people present here, see, her hands are now mine, let this marriage prove auspicious.

This song simulates the *Mangalashtak* sung in Hindu marriages, and may be correctly called a *Mangal Panchak.*

While the new couple moves around the auspicious objects in the pandal, this song is sung:

Saaee gor gor umaa daadaa aavaal
Soon gar gaar umaa ga
Baalle chudoor in maa daadaa aavaale
Vaalle felaa inmaaa ga
Faalaa zaap vaataa daadaa aavaalaa
Naalee laacheke kitaa gaa
Navaa vashikaa mandaa daadaa aavaal
Bijaad baajaad Otaa gaa

Kure kaalhe mandaa daadaa vaalaa
Maal muhoore mandaa gaa
Pitte mendul mandaa daadaa aavaal
Ponee leg mandaa gaa.

Meaning

O dada, (Bridegroom) do not take away my vahini (The bride) away from the altar. Do not consider her very young or old. Take quick steps. See her blooming breasts, beautiful deer like legs, peacock-like face and body like a parrot. Her sound is like a slowly burning wick of a lantern.

Sentiments on Separation

While returning back after the marriage the bride is weeping and her relatives are feeling very bad.

On that occasion this song is sung.

Paaro ingaa saa saahote
Mivaa teree daure
Khaalvo saahote
Bhaaee lolaa daure
Nevaa teree nivaa koraate doure
Chudaare usaaree pitte dounaa karaate
Dounaa koraataal partiyaale usaarpitte
Zado zaadee alaal
Chudoo re usaar pitte
Yaayaana koraate
Yaayaaanaa kortaal pireetaale usaarpitte
Zaado zaadee alaai
Chudoore usaar pitte
Daadaanaa koraate
Daadaanaa kortaal pireetaale usaarpitte
Zaado zaadee alaal.

Meaning

O, Baba, affection has no parallel,

people's love is deceptive.
Today is the last day when I am getting your company.
Henceforth I will have to stay amidst unknown people. This beautiful sparrow (the bride) was living under loving umbrella of her father. Now she is flying away. She will go to the jungle and weep. Until now she was in the warm protection of her mother. Now she is flying away and will weep. Uptill now she was under her brother's protection, now she will fly away and weep.

This song very nicely depicts the sentiments of the bride's relatives and can be compared with similar songs sung in the modern world.

This is an amorous song. After the marriage ceremony, the turmeric applied to the body is cleansed after which the groom can take away the bride to any place.

The groom's sister says:

Tedaa bhabhee de
Kor kustaa, faal vaaleetaa
Tedaa bhaabhee de
Teda siyor vo
Kaeenpaaro kaaee vaaltor
Tedaa siyor vo
Kaad paaro kaal vaaltor
Teda siyor vo
Teda bhaabhee de.

Meaning

O, Vahini, get up. The cock is crowing.
Day has dawned. Get up quickly.
How can I get up my husband is not allowing me, his hand is on my body. His legs are also on my body. He doesn't allow me to get up.
O'Bhabhi, Get up.

A Song Teasing Bhabhi (Brother's Wife)

After the bride enters the marriage pandal her feet are washed. On this occasion teasing, amorous songs or even vulgar songs are also sung. See this example.

Vaaldee pisiyaa bhaabhee
Jaldee pisiyaa de
Anaa varonge bhavarayaanaa
Vaatonaa de de.
Maanee makamaa bhaabhee manee makamaa de
Aanaa chaudharayaal sottaaree
Vaatonaa de de.
Maanee vareemaa bhabhee maanee sodeemaade
Jaldee pasiyaa bhaabhee
Jaldee pasiyaa de.
Dhodaang Mattaang vaatee ho pale kaamaang vittee ho
Bohaa poharataa yer uttee, dare bhaabhee dare
Yer sehor maataa de.
Nivaa paatvaan jaavaane vaatonaa ho
Naake bichchonaa vaataa, dare bhaabhee dare
Kaal miheechee sim dhaare, bhabhee dare
Kaal saahore maata ree
Thaathore bangalaa vo bonaa ro
He baapoo, He raajaa ro, baangataa hulashee raamtonaa de
He raane he, he laadee de, baanglaat paaro nava hi gala de
Naavaa hee galaa de.

Hid haugalaa bahadoor dena de
Miyaan ige bor borvaasee ro lelatulaa
Miyaan ige hutoomal vaasee ro paalaatulaa
Miyaan ige dhokume vaasi ro paalaa tollaa
Miyaan ige Mhasolaal vaasi ro paalaatulaa
Miyaan ige gadhaalayaava vaasee ro paalaatulaa
Miyan ige bor bor vaasee ro paalaatulaa.

Meaning

"O Bhabhi come out of the house.

I am infatuated towards you. Don't try to hide yourself. I have brought a special thing for you. You have come from a mountainous area, from the river. You have eaten the tender shoots of the *Salai* (*Bosvellia serrata*) tree."

"I have became your lover please prepare a bed for me. The liquor of your love has reached my head and I am soaked in it. You also join me."

"O boy who had come to your mother?
Camel, Jackal, Buffalo or donkey?
It seems you have received their impression marks."

Marriage Songs of the Kolam

During the marriage ceremony the bride's party and the groom's party cut jokes with each other. For example this song.

Amme pilla kandkad

Amme Pilla Kandkad, Amme Pilla Kandkad
Mograknet Puvvakisha, Puvvabarabar Kandkad
Imme Bala Kandkan, Imme Bala Kandkan
Shihuknet Khuthekisha, Khutebarabar Kandkan
Amme Pilla Kandkad, Amme Pilla Kandkad.

Kavarane Ruikishya, Sevvake Ruyyi Yena Kandkad
Imme Bala Kandkan, Imme Bala Kandkan
Mulolito Muloli Gini, Khubi dayyuk Kandkan
Amme Pillane Mungalal, Amme Pillane Mungalal
Koya, Koya Mungalal, Yenang Shobhittana Kandkan.

Imme Balane Mungalal, Imme Balane Mungalal
Ir`Unakad Habshikisha, Habshilang Kandkad
Amme Pilla Kandkad, Amme Pilla Kandkad
Lakshmi Ani Durga Devilang Kandkad

Imme Lala Kandkan, Imme Lala Kandkan
Mahabharat te Bhimkisha, Bhimbarabar Kandkan.
Amme Pilla Andan, Amme Pilla Andad
Hushar te Hushar gini Ovvol Oleng Kandkad

Gebbuk te Gebbuk gini, Oleng Kandkan
Imme Bala Kandkan, Imme Bala Kandkan.

Meaning

The bride's parents are praising the girl and at the same time teasing the bridegroom. Our girl is like the delicate flower of *Mogra* and the fragrance of her youth is attracting all. While your son is like the straight trunk of a *Khair* tree and is hard like a soldier.

The girl is fair and looks white like cotton while your boy looks like skeleton and is black in colour.

The nose of our daughter is just becoming to her face while your son's nose is like the handle of a water pump.

Our daughter looks like Laxmi or Goddess Durga, while your son looks like Bal Bhima from Mahabharat that means he is ugly.

Our daughter is not only beautiful but also useful for domestic work. As compared to her, your son is a dullard and of low qualities.

The Kankan Song

These songs are sung at the time of the culmination of marriage ceremony, when the ritual thread on the wrist is taken out.

Usurka Poroka
Aam Babu Parakan
Aam Babu Olane
Kaknyal Sasyure

Meaning

The leaves of Amla tree, our babu walks by rubbing his stomach.
Our babu is looking, take out the bangles from his hands.

Another Kankan song

Dada, Aam Dada Olatun
Kaknya Saso
Doi, Aam Doi Olatun
Kaknya Saso

Meaning

We look at our Dada,
He should take out our bangle,
We look at our grandmother,
She should take out our bangles.

Korku Marriage Songs

Songs Addressed to the Bride

Are mansat renjo
Chaare mansat renjo
Besaayo raajaaji
Aaja man kaakaa ke
Bulayo raajaaji,
Aaye man bhaaye ke
Bulayo raajaaji, besaayo raajaaji ...1
Kodo man nando
Bulayo raajaaji
Baata man chitaa
Udaayo raajaaji, besaayo raajaaji ...2
Sone ke nivalo
Khilaayo raajaaji
Rupaye ke pyalo
Pillaayo raajaaji, besaayo raajaaji ...3

Meaning

This song is addressed to the bride.

"O, bride don't be nervous and annoyed. This bridegroom has been approved by your uncle, brother and all others.

He will give you to eat in a golden bowl and water in a silver glass.

All women and girls sing these songs collectively on the occasion of marriage.

Go s s go s s doraani, go s s go s s doraani
Gaangulaa gaadaan koko gaa kadobaa

Go s s go s s do s s raanee,
Aa s s maani tankula le jaave hendo
Ee s s nee jaalee kendaave,
Go s s go s s do raanee ...1
Bo s s do s s raanee, bo s s doraani baaree,
Haaree bodo s s
Rodo s bo s s bo s s do s raanee baaro haaree
Go s s go s s raanee ...2
Aa s s maanee s s iso yendoy yendo,
Ee s s nee s paisa le khabe s s
Go s s go s s raanee ...3

Meaning

The bridegroom says, "O, my Rani (queen) look! We shall go to the river to catch fish, O, Rani let us go to the lake to catch fish. We shall take fish with us and go to the market. There we will get twenty rupees (by selling the fish).

This song is in praise of the house where the bride is going.

Endo malee re endo maalee
Lakhpatee ghar me beti ko diyo
Endo maalee ...1
Aadha chaandee re, aadha sona
Lakhpatee gharme beti ko diyo re ...2

Meaning

The girl is going to a house which is of a man who is a man of lakhs. In her house half the house is full of gold and half is full of silver.

Song of the Groom

Jogee jaate hain lodonee
Kaise le, kaise le
Mharo to nand ke raajaa,
Aamne to kavnaa bade chale
Kaise le, kaise le ...1
Aamne tomne baaran singanee

Mor sikane nand ke raajaa
Raanee nand chale
Kaise le, kaise le ...2

Meaning

O, Jogi (bridegroom) where are you going?
This Nandraja is going to his house (Bada).
The Rani (bride) is also going in *Barat* to the place of Nandraja who is walking like a peacock.

Another Song

Shankarjee ke liye maine bhojan pakayo
Bhojan pakayo
Shankarjee khelan kare
Kiyen ko na bole
Ghar me tere khele

Meaning

I have prepared meals for Lord Shankar (Shiva).
Lord Shankar is playing in your courtyard. Don't tell others.

Song on Bride-price

Gaangulya gaangulya dodo s s maa
Gaangulya do s s s do s ma s
Gaangulya gom s aay gaangulya
domay inje torave
Konje tore maay aam do s s do ...1
Jonje log tore maay, do s s do
Konje murto dodo s s s do s s ...2

Meaning

Bridegroom says, "I have not yet seen the figure of the girl (bride) but huge money has been taken from me for her (as bride-price)".

When ritual starts this song is sung.

Gaangaaro gaangaa ro, chobeesa gaangaaro
Dain gaangaaro re s s ...1
Shobha, aavo ye raanee,
Devadeebhar phulonnaa, tode vo raanee
Gaangaaro gaangaaro re s s ...2

Meaning

O, friends come, let us cleanse the floor.
O, Shobha Rani, pluck flowers for the worship.

The Groom Persuading the Bride

Chalo raanee vo chalo raanee, chalo raanee
Apanaa jaanaa door hai, chalo raanee
Dera raajaa, dera raajaa
Mera gahana pahanoongee
Chalo raanee ...1
Ekhee maanyala theko raajaa
Mere mayase miloongee
Chalo raanee ...2
Tere mayase kya mile raanee
Mera ghoda nahee thaave
Chalo raanee ...3

Meaning

The bridegroom is eagerly persuading the bride to accompany him. He says, "O, Rani, come on quickly".

The bride says, "O, Raja, let me put on my ornaments. Let me once meet my mother, then shall come".

The bridegroom says, "Why do you meet your mother now, start quickly, my horse is impatient and unable to wait any more, come quickly".

When the bride starts for going to the bridegroom's place, the women from the bride side sing this song.

Rainee ma rainee buroo rainee
Rainee itaang kuva laage

Plate 1: Madia Women Dancing: bon-fire seen in the foreground.— Photo by Ravi Joshi

Plate 2: Korku Children Singing *'Dedra-Mata Paani De'* at Village Khaparkheda near Dharni — *Photo by* Dr. Deogaonkar

Plate 3: Korku Tribals from Pastalai near Dharni Dancing at Rand-Bhave Festival. — *Photo by* Dr. Deogaonkar

Plate 4: Madia Boys dancing, tossing a scare-crow in the air, touch of modernity is perceptible. — *Photo by* Ravi Joshi

Plate 5: A Group of Madia Women ready to dance. Mark their ornaments. — *Photo by* Dr. Deogaonkar

Plate 6: Madia men from Kachler (near Etapalli) dancing around Bon-Fire. — *Photo by* Sibi Alex

Plate 7: A Group of Madia girls, ready for a dance. On extreme right is the author Dr. Shailaja Deogaonkar. Mark their ornaments

— *Photo by* Ravi Joshi

Plate 8: Madia men in traditional attire in a dancing pose. — *Photo by* Ravi Joshi

Plate 9: A group of elderly Madia women in traditional dress, ready to start dancing. — *Photo by* Ravi Joshi.

Plate 10: At village Vasamundi — two Madia Tribals displaying their traditional musical instruments near their Ghotul. From Left (back-line) Pagai, Kundudi and Dhol. In the fore-ground are three Chitkoras. — *Photo by* Dr. Deogaonkar

Sone kee chumadee rupaye ka ghadaa
Kisaan kee ladakee, kain jaaee paanee bhare?
Apano raa, dudaa vetaa
Kisaan konjee kee cheej bole, kounjaai paanee bhare?
Tutaa mendokee maanjee maay do s s do
Iyaan jugunoo Dharanee se gagaa aave paanee bhare.

Meaning

O, Raini, who is standing near the well?
With a golden *chumbal* on the head and a silver pot?
Who is this, farmer's daughter? Our daughter, shining like a glow-worm is coming from Dharni for taking water.

Bride's Affection for the Parents

Haje maan jo, haje maa
Haje maan jo ladaee lee re
Eyan na raan haje, ladaee lee re
Aamaa lee no sadee ko saadee
Eve redho ladaee lee
Chokharaa ten maa eve rejaa, ladaee lee re
Eyaan me jaa baa raa baraso
Ba yaado haje vaa, ladaee lee re.

Meaning

The bridegroom asks the bride to come to him after putting on the sari given by him.

The bride says, she will not put on his sari as she remembers her parents, hence I shall put on my old saree given by my parents.

Banjara Marriage Songs

Turmeric Songs

Songs while applying turmeric powder to the groom

Veera mote sherem jaau kair?

Veera nav mal haldi mol laau kair!
Veera husheti haldi lagau kair ...1

Veera mote sherem jaau kair
Veera nav mal saakharya laau kair.
Veera gundi laaduri pangat varaadu kair ...2

Veera mote sherem jaau kair
Veera nav mal kukoo laau kair
Veera husheti kukoo lagaau kair ...3

Meaning

At her brother's marriage the sister sings this song. She says "Shall I go to the market and bring nine mounds of turmeric and apply it to your body?"

Again she asks, "Shall I bring nine mounds of sugar from market and serve *Bundi ladoo* (Sweet balls) at the marriage feast?"

Lastly she asks, "Shall I fetch nine mounds of kumkum from market for your marriage?

Turmeric, sugar and *ladoo* as well as kumkum are all auspicious things at marriage and the unit of nine mounds also indicates her auspicious blessings, as number 'nine' is supposed to be an auspicious figure in the Hindus.

Taangdeer Song, Sung While Applying Turmeric Powder to the Bride

Chhodiyaake aaee yadis
Ek ghadi laageto, so ghadi
Laagayach yaadee ...1

Mare ke baablaree choonkeree chaavodee
Chaavodees hidoo yaavodees ...2

Mariyeke virenaaro Limboovaaro baag
Limboo aam todee yaarodees ...3

Meaning

Mother you have left me at my husband's place, I am feeling one minute as one hundred minutes.

My father's drawing room/office is well built. I stroll in it (I feel like returning to take a stroll in his room).

My brother's garden is full of lemon trees, I feel like coming to the garden and plucking lemons in the garden.

This song depicts the mind of a married girl, who though in her husband's house often remembers her parents, brother etc.

Song Sung while Giving Feast on Engagement

Raadha – mithi ghodali,
Ran – mithi talawar,
Sej – mithi kaamini,
Sura – mithi saang,
Lo Bhai Bhang.

Meaning

A mare is liked by a warrior (Radha – a brave man or warrior), a sword is liked while going to war and hunting, a woman is liked while going to bed, similarly, O'friends, treat this feast as dear to you and start taking food and Bhang. (Hemp)

Bride's Feelings on Separation from Parents

Chhut giyaaye maari baapuri haveli
Khaayeshi piveshi nangri
Mari Nayak Bapuri nangri;
Gujrathni yaadi
Umariyav baapu
Kesariya Viranna,
Havel chhodiyaali yaadi.

Meaning

I am leaving my father's house. The house where I was well-fed is being left by me. I am leaving our Naiks village. My mother is Gujrathan (a lady from Gujarat) father is an Urmao, my brother is a brave Kesariya and I am leaving all of them.

Medi Peetee — Songs Sung while Grinding Mehandi (*Lawsonia inermis*)

Medidal medidal chay laada
Leriyaa peesaa dicheek koneere
Aadleem peesa ee jeev kasaa ...1

Khoto peesa chaale neere
Bana peesar, Raani maleneere
Lereeya pesa dicheek koneere ...2

Meaning

We are grinding Mehandi for marriage, does the wolf give money or not (Wolf indicates the groom). Our mind is like money in a measuring pot. As counterfeit coins don't work, so also bride cannot be obtained without money. Does the wolf pay money or not?

The above song shows the existence of the practice of bride-price.

Another Song

Matayake karoya Naayakaa yaadee
Yadee dek baapu dekay laajoo maar, naakore
Lakopatee jivadaa ...1
Aadee raavot aageli poree raavot, peechedi yaadee ...2
Aalaa modee, kulaa modee, kul modee
Haa-them zaari len paaneeyan jaavoo yaadee ...3

Meaning

Oh, Naik mother, see how I am shy of father, my life is of lakhs worth.

Ahead of me there are many girls and behind me also there are girls, and behind me is my brother.

My style of walking is unique. I am going to fetch water with a brass pot.

Festival Songs

Festivals and Festive Moods

Different festivals are associated with different seasons. Before the advent of rains and after the first showers of rain there are *Poojas* and festivals. Similarly before harvest and after the harvest there are festivals. *Amavasya* (No-moon day) and *Poornima* (Full-moon day) from particular Hindu months are celebrated. Dussera, Holi are important traditional festivals in many tribes like the Gonds, the Korkus etc. Diwali is also adopted as a festival of lights. Some festivals are glorifying brother-sister relationship like the Jeroti in the Korkus. There are songs for all these festivals which are based on themes connected with the festivals or may be on spiritual themes, praise of Gods or Nature, origin of mankind and the Universe, bravery etc. or depicting amorous love, husband-wife relations, material wants of life and even songs containing abuses.

Gondi/Madia Gonds Songs

Dussera Festival

For the Madia-Gonds Dussera is an important festival. It is celebrated at Patti level and on the Vijaya Dashmi day all Madias and Gonds assemble at Aheri Maharajas palace.

On Dussera day while going to Aheri to their traditional Gond king—the Aheri Zamindar—they dance and sing this song. It is almost like a marching song. *Tina Namur, nei namur* is a special style of dancing.

Re-Reelo … Re-reelo s s s
Tinā nāmur, nei nāmur, Ho s s Ho s s
Tedānā uddānā
Mavor bābānā derā
Tinā nāmur, nei nāmur
Nei namur … Nānā-Titi s s s
Aheri nate Jimmedār (Zamindar), Rām Rām bolo
Tedānā uddānā
Mavor bābānā derā

Tinā-nāmur, nei nāmur ... Ho ... Ho Re-Reela

Meaning

Sitting, standing, sitting standing Ho, Ho s s
Our camp is marching in a group to our King.
Sitting, standing we are going to our Zamindars' (kings') place—Aheri
To wish him *Ram Ram* (to pay our respects to him)
Our king's camp is thus marching ahead,
Sitting, standing, Ho ... Ho s s s

The content and words in such songs change from village to village and from person to person. Songs from villages near Marathi speaking areas show a strong Marathi influence, while those from near the Bastar border show a Hindi influence.

A Gondi Song

A song sung in praise of Lingo during Diwali festival is given below:

Rena s s Rena s s s Re s s
Savri Mara Aakita Koya Saga Wata
Johar Jo Nivay Muth Lingo Baba
Udi Aaki Savrita Udam Saga Wata

Meaning

O'God Lingo you organised our Gond (Koya) community like the Katsavri tree*. O'God Lingo, we salute and worship you for ordering our Gond Saga (Gotra—clans) in an orderly manner like the Katsavri tree.

Nature

At the time of festivals they sing songs on nature, rains, birds, etc. See the following songs.

* Katsavri tree (*Bombax malabaricum*) has profuse branching. A typical feature is its seeds spread through air like parachutes. This simulates the spread or fanning out of Gond clans, ordained by Lingo.

On Rains and Hailstorm

Vadiyu vāta phiru vātā
Bandang aranta, Hooda Hooda!
Bandang tintu, bandang tintu
Phiru vata, phiru vata

Meaning

Wind comes, rain comes. Hailstones fall, look look. Eat hailstones, eat hailstones. Rain comes, rain comes.

A song on a parrot sitting on a mango tree.

Markā marāte rāgo utāro, nanā rāgo hudtānā
Bore Dādi shobhā yeshitorh, nanā rāgo hudtānā
Rama Dādi shobhā yeshitorh, nanā rāgo hudtāna
Markā marāte rago utāro, nanā rago hudtāna

Meaning

The parrot is sitting on the mango tree, Yes, I too have seen it. Let me see who (which man) kills it. Oh, I have seen Rama has killed it. I have seen the parrot sitting on the mango tree.

A Madia-Gondi song sung during festive mood reflects their love and observation of nature.

Ree Reelo s s , Reelo s s s
Keyom Keyom Ke, Keyom Keyom Ke
Keyom Keyom Ke, Keyom Ke s s Yonge
Aalo Devane Ye s s s Lole
Nettur — dara Pod-duye
Pod-duyelo Pod-duye, Keyom Keyom Ke
Kamka – dara Lenjuye
Lenjuyelo Len s s Juye, Keyom Keyom Ke
Kanda Kadwo Ittaye
Ittayelo Ittayelo s s s Ittaye
Kamaboya Ta s diye
Tadiyelo Taa s diye
Keyom Keyom Ke, Keyom Keyom Ke s s s Yonge

Meaning

'Keyon Keyom Ke' is an imitation of peacocks sound. O sister, colour of the Sun is reddish like blood. Colour of the Moon is yellow like turmeric. O sister, the branches and leaves of tamarind tree are grouping and hence through them one cannot see the colour of Sun or Moon.

But, O sister the leaves of Toddy tree are sparse and hence one can see the colour of the Sun and Moon.

If we look at the above song from literary point of view the similes are really appealing. Similarly the alliteration is also worth noting. Moreover the sound of the peacock is nicely placed to form the last line of every quadruplicate. It can also be sung very well.

Some songs are sung in the form of question and answers. These give information. For example;

Re s s Reelo, s s s Reelo s s Re s s
Aatal Batal Banduk Injore?
Tunde Badga Banduk Injore.
Aatal Batal Aangris Injore?
Naiyur Iska Aangris Injore.
Aatal Batal Pula Injore?
Pindigudam Pula Injore.
Aatal Batal Bhaire Injore?
Pindigudam Maur Injroe.

Meaning

Of what is the Gun (Banduk) made of?
The gun is made of the wood of *Tunda* tree.
Of what is the gun-powder made of?
The gun-powder (Barud) is made of sand.
Of what is the vegetable (Pula) prepared?
Vegetable is made of Pindigudam (a fat of animal).
Of which animal the hunting is going on?
The hunting is of the Pindigudanm (animal).

A Love Song

This is a Gondi song which uses many similes based on objects from nature to describe the youth for a maiden.

Re l a a s s Ree Ree la
Nāvā ré s s s
Nāvāre chyāte markā marā
Markā marā wārun wātāré
Āli shringār dole wātā
Re relo, Relā .. s s ... Ree Relaa s s ... 1
Nāvare chyāte limbu marā
Limbu marā wārun wātāré
Āli shringār dole wātā
Relā ... Ree Relā Re s s ...2
Nāvāre chyāte sitāmarā
Sitāmarā wārun wātāre
Āli shringār dole wātā
Relā ... Ree Relā R .. s s s ...3
Nāvāre chyate shitimarā
Rengā marā wārun wātāre
Āli shringār dole wātā
Re-relo Relā s s Re-relaā s s ...4
Nāvāre jwāni mantā
Haushā! tu ran hidā mantā?
Relā Ree Rela s s Relā s s s ...5

The song which is a very popular one among the Madia boys and girls may be broadly translated as under.

1. Oh my dear lover see my garden. Look at this mango tree. How rich it has become with full grown mangoes! This tree is beautifully cradling on the breezes of the air.
2. Look at this lemon tree. This is laden with nice lemons and is gracefully moving due to gentle breezes.
3. Look at this custard-apple tree (*sitaphal*). This tree also is full of fruits and is gently moving on both sides and looks beautiful.
4. Oh, dear, look at this chrysanthemum plant. It is full of fragrant flowers. It looks very charming while swaying on the breeze.

5. Isn't my youthfulness like these trees? Oh, my dear, where are you?

Polo

Tribal folk-songs show a capacity to adapt new themes, forms and dimensions. *Polo* (election) creates enthusiasm and a festive mood.

Election period is also a social occasion for the Madia. They turn up in good numbers. Songs are also sung in Relas based on the elections. See this specimen.

(Here *Polo* means election)

Dā dā dā, hike polo mantā
Vā, vā, vā, hike vāi ro ... Re Relo s s
Hille kabād kisi mantā
Hudā, Hudā, Hudā, idu pattete vatānā
Kagidi mantā
Idu kāgidi poyasi lopattā
Arrā ne hann ....
Vāi ro, vāiro, bāi miku bonku
Chiti watānā mantā
Hudā, hudā, idu hille kabād kisi mantā
Onā chinā porrā idu chāpā kimtu
Vāiro ... vāi ... Re Rela s s s

Meaning

Come, come. Look. Here is election. All work is done: (You have no work to do) Look, look, look, you will get a ballot-paper; put it in ballot-box and cast your vote. Come on, vote for the person of your choice, but he must be an able and good man. Put the stamp against the symbol of such a person.

Songs of the Kolam

A festival called *Kargul* is celebrated on the *Nagpanchami* day. This song is sung on the occasion hence called '*Kargul* song'.

Shili Modal, Moduk Modal
Aare Rama Raghoba Re!

Teke Modal, Madgi Modal! Aareo...........
Sitta Modal, Meli Modal! Aareo............
Ranga Modal, Burra Modal! Aareo............

Like this the song may be continued by adding the names of various trees and ending by 'Aare Rama Raghoba Re'.

Another festival song teasing the Bhagat (priest) is given below:

Nevali Bhete Kave Miyada
Taneda Miyada Taneda Toda?
Supari Save Seddina
Miya Tiragad Yenar!

Meaning

The tortoise is grazing on the banks of river. We do not know as to, on what it is grazing.
The Bhagat's belly has gone down, hence, they say, he is grazing.

Festival Songs of the Korku

Holi is an important festival for the Korku. Holi falls in the Hindu month of *Phalgun* and hence called Phagnai songs and in the Korku dialect *Sirinj* means a song.

Holi/Phagnai Sirinj (Holi songs)

Nimo maryo tere ban me,
Nim – maryo tere ban me
Nim maryo tere pas
Wo chaliyo, dharni-ke lal
Loot liyo re
tere Ban me

I am lost in your forest. I am coming to you. O friend, dear son of the earth, you have looted; I am lost in your forest.

Story of Creation of Mankind

The song tells us how the Gods assembled to create mankind.

Herom Hera Baso Malaye
Serom Sera Mankayro
Hero Ka upar lalo Malaye
Heroya Jambu Mora Re ...1

Aagso Doge Dhuwandhar Do
Dharti Doge Kadapan
Abhyanindma Surato Ban
Abhyanindma Murato Ban ...2

Chetiskoti Dewataku Dundiya Joda
Chatanni Ja Subun Ken
Chetiskoti Dewataku Choja Mansuba tolemal
Kagaliya Masase usana mati
Aasini kule-bheja, kagaliya masa
Deriya tapun sene chalya AafiReja;
Banayo dane, murto ban do.

This is a traditional song explaining the origin of mankind. When 36 crore Gods assembled under a Banyan tree and decided to create mankind they sent the crow, *viz.*, Kagbhusandji (Kagliya Masa) who had to fly a long distance for getting earth and had to lose its feathers also. Ultimately the crow succeeded in getting earth from Goddess 'Deemak Devi' (termite) who asked him to return the earth after the purpose is over. The crow agreed. The Gods then prepared idols of man and woman and poured life in them. The man is buried after death because the clay is to be returned as per promise given by the crow to Deemak Devi.

Hero ma Hero Waso malaye
Serom Sera mankayro
Hero Ka upar lalo malaye
Heroya Jambu Morare

Aagaso Dekhe kala chando
Dharetu Dekhe Dhuwa chale
Hero Ka upar lalo malaye
Heroya Jambu Morare

Banaya Dane Surato Ban do
Banayo Dane murato Ban do
Hero Ka upar lal malaye
Heroya Jambu Morare

Before creation, there was only a shade prepared from green bamboos and covered with green *Jamun* leaves and branches. In the sky the moon was black and the earth was covered with smoke or dew. Small fruits of *Jamun* tree were shining like small red beads. But there was no life – *i.e.*, living creatures on earth.

The conceptualisation of the Universe at the time of creation depicted in this song is laudable. Black sky and gaseous earth roughly simulates the scientific knowledge known today. *Jamun* tree seems to be of primitive existence.

During the Holi festival they drink liquor and dance and invite all to join its celebration. Purna is a big and auspicious river for them. The Korku were previously under Rajput Chieftains – Maharajas. They are also remembered and respected in songs.

Aare bala aao, Purname phagun khele
Khele Maharaj;
Aao Purname Holi phagun khele
Rani Chali woke, Mayaka me o Lal
Raja chale, sasural,
Are bala Purname phagun khele
Ranike hatho-me Gulab ki Chadiya
Rajaka hatho-me Kamal,
Aare bala Purname phagun khele.
Raja bethere houda, Rani bethere havadar
Aare bala Purname phagun khele.

Meaning

Maharaj (King) is playing *Holi* in Purna (River by name Purna) but Rani (Queen) has started for her mother's place. Maharaj is also following her to his mother-in-law's place. Rani has a rose flower in her hand while the Maharaj is having a lotus flower in his hand. Rani sitting in a palanquin and Maharaj sitting on the back of elephant is playing *Holi* in Purna.

Kanhaiya, i.e. Lord Shrikrishna and holy rivers are also remembered. See this song.

Kanhaiyalal tune mhari ghagar phode
Kanhaiyalal tune mhari ghagar phode

Etpar Ganga, Utpar Jamuna
Bichame Jamuna Bharaye, Nandlal
tune mhari ghagar phode ...1

Jamuna ke neer tir, gauva charaye
Bichame Sakhiya nache, Nandlal
tune mhari ghagar phode ...2

Meaning

Oh, deer Kanhaiya (Krishna) you have broken my water-pot. On one side is Ganga and on the other is Yamuna (rivers) and Yamuna is in spates and O, Kanhaiya you have broken my water-pot.

On the banks of Yamuna (your) cows are grazing and in the midst the girl friends are dancing, O Nandlal (son of Nand, *i.e.* Krishna) you have broken my water-pot. Influence of Hindi is clearly seen in the above two songs.

One more Holi song is given below. These are also called *Horiyar Sirinj*.

The poetic imagination springs high on such festive occasions and on looking, at a beautiful lady, a song flows out.

Description of a beautiful lady

The Korku concept of an ideal beautiful lady is reflected in the following song where the girl (*Mala*) is addressed as a Gondoni, *i.e.* a Gond woman and hence the name is Malai-Gondoni.

Jaisa bana tinjken, Malai Gondoni do
Jaisa bana tinjken, Malai Gondoni re . . . 1

Amani tingdi do, Malai Chojama do
Jaisa bana tinjken, Malai Gondoni re

Kedani Khambo nido ama tengdi mado
Jaisa bana ...

Amani bulu do, Malai Chajani do
Jaisa bana ...

Tekla jeni poptani do, jama bulum do
Jaisa bana ...

Amani bhujani do, Malai chojani do
Jaisa bana ...

Chanini lato nido Malai bhujama do
Jaisa bana ...

Amani chabo nido Malai Chojani do
Tambra burujni do, abha chunuma do
Jaisa bana ...

Amani bhu nido Malai chojama do
Jaisa bana ...

Ravani chachu Keja, abha muni do
Jaisa bana

Charmurk petyani, abha gala ma do
Jaisa bana ...

Amani met nido, Malai chojama do
Jaisa bana ...

Chandoma Surjo Keja, abha metni do
Jaisa bana ...

The beautiful woman Malai Gondoni is hand pounding grains by pounding stump in the hollow pounding stone and its rhythmic sound is coming. She has put on a nice *petticoat, Challa* (ring) in finger and a nice blouse. This woman is looking still more beautiful as she is pounding grains.

'Tinjken' is an onomatopoeic sound of the pounding work.

This song is in question-answer sequence. Every time a question is put as to how a particular part of the body is looking? An answer is given by using metaphor. The sequence is as follows:

Her legs and thighs are like the soft yellowish stem (trunk) of a Banana tree, her nose is like a parrot, her arms are looking like waves of water (as she is pounding vigorously with arms), her face is like red watermelon, her cheek are like chironji pieces, and her eyes are shining like Moon and Sun. She is pounding in a rhythmic movement, 'Tinjken, Tinjken'. The literary and poetic values are very rich.

Banjara Festival Songs

Nagpanchmi Song: A Sister is Appealing to her Brother

Virelaa kabase khadeere dukanpar
Virelaa haaslo daraare taare raajem
Virelaa baapuri kilalee taare haatem
Virelaa haaslo daraare taare raajem
Virelaa ghaalan heendee taare baagem
Virelaa kabase khadeera dukanpar
Virelaa bhureeya daraare taare raajem
Virelaa ghaalan hindu taare baagem
Virelaa ghaalan hindu taare raajem
Virelaa kabase khadeere dukanpar
Virelaa lovadee daraare taare raajem
Virelaa ondan hindu taare baagem
Virelaa odan hindure taare raajem

Baaeeye baarataalee jou oree vaataye
Baaeeye sutevutero oro thaataye
Baaeeye baapu melee Posaden
Baaeeye daselagu joou ori vataye
Baaeeye redu ghadeero oro thataye
Baapu Posaden go ma bolee konee
Baapu lovadee laaye ma bolee konee
Virelaa bare meenaaro san aayore
Virelaa baaeen balaau aayore
Virelaa baaee saaroo lovaadee laayore
Virelaa lovaadee pasand konee aaee re
Vivelaa lovadee husetee laayore
Vivelaa bhavaj dekach risetore.

Meaning

O Dada, I am standing in your shop for a long time.
O Dada, please give me a *mala* of beads.
O Dada, the key of father's safe is with you so, please utilise your power and give me the *mala* of beads.
O Dada, I shall roam in the garden after putting on the *mala*

around my neck.
O Dada, I am standing in your shop for a pretty long time.
O Dada, give me the nose ring. I shall put on that nose ring and roam in the garden.
O Dada, I shall put on the *mala* of beads and roam in your domain.
O Dada, I am waiting in your shop for a long time. Please give me an Odhani. I shall put on the *Odhani* and move in your garden.
O Tai, send Dada to the Bazar at Pusad.
O Tai, we shall wait for Dada till 12 O'clock.
O Tai, Dada has put on suit and boots and is looking up-to-date.

Tai, let us send Dada to Pusad we shall sit for him till 10 O'clock.

Tai, he likes radio and watch very much. Baba went to Pusad but I could not talk to him. Baba has brought *Odhani* but I am not talking with him.

Dada, the festival has come after 12 months. Dada, come along with Tai. Dada has come with clothes for Tai, but she dislikes the clothes. Dada has brought clothes very gladly.

But Dada, Wahini (Dada's wife) is looking at me angrily.

This song is sung at Dussera *festival.*

Sudaa savaaye bhaktoo peree
Kaache keree divaalo
Karpoor veeve aaratee me
Mek melaaree aaratee me
Pavane paanee aaratee me
Chande sutaaree aaratee me
Jaanee maataa aaratee me

Meaning

O, beautiful Goddess, I am your devotee standing at your doors. I am burning camphor for your aarti. I pray Moon, Sun and mother and request them to give us good rains.

This is a song which is sung at the time of Holi festival

Aaore daayasaanee holeer khelaa
Baar meenaam aaeer holee holee
Khelor zoketee ...1
Holee khelore raaj jalam dinor
Holee khelor zoketee ...2

Meaning

All old men please come.
We shall celebrate Holi. Holi comes only once after twelve months.
Let us, celebrate Holi at leisure.
Lord Rama has given us birth, hence let us celebrate Holi at leisure.

Saint Sevadas or Sevabhaya is worshipped by all Banjaras. This song is addressed to him, and sung at Holi.

Kaaee chhoder goroon sevaalaatol
Poharaagad vase pado ...1
Haafaa badoon sobatam lido
Hole garaasyaa saadairee dholee haavoree ...2
Poharaagadh vase pado, Navase dharen sobatem lido
Kaaee ladenee laador sevaalaal ...3
Poharaa gad vase pado.

Meaning

O Sevadas Maharaj, why did you leave the Banjara people. Because you left, your native place Pohragad has become deserted.

Your brother along with Hafa Bandu left Poharagad and took along with him Garsha Sand (Bull) and cows and Pohragad became deserted.

O Sevabhaya, you left along with the people from Navse household on a tour and O Bhagwant (God), your Pohragad became deserted.

Draupadi Song

This song is sung by Draupadi and she is sincerely calling Lord Shrikrishna.

Haakaaroo re kaanaavirelaa kalakaleetee
Bharee sabhaamaaee hubeere kaanaavirelaa
Man kavar gher lidere kaanaavirelaa
Maar ijjat rakaadare kanaavirelaa ... 1
Man saadee puraadare kaanaavirelaa
On anteekaranetee haakaaroore kaanaavirelaa
Gaadee durakaatee aajor kaanaavirelaa
Haakaroore kaanaavirelaa kalakaleetee ... 2

Meaning

O Kanhadada (brother Shrikrishna), I called you most sincerely. I am standing alone in the assembly surrounded by the Kauravas. Please, save my modesty and honour.

O Kanhadada, supply me saree. I am calling you from the bottom of my heart.

O Kanha, you come quickly from Dwarka, I am calling you from the bottom of my heart.

Lord Vithoba's Worship Song

Soneree vitep hubore vitthalaa Pandhareem neto
Bel fuleree maal laaeere Vitthalaa devalem beto
Pedha naarel laaeere Vitthalaa devalem beto
Janaabaaeen ghatee pisaaye Vitthalaa devalem beto
Meeraabaaen jer pachaayer Vitthalaa devalem beto
Saavataa maaleen bhaajee khudaaye Vitthalaa devalem beto
Gorya kumbharen gaaraa khundaayo Vitthalaa devalem beto
Bhakteem baalaa khundaayo Vitthalaa devalem beto
Taare bhakten paayore – Vitthala Pandhaareem beto
Ham Kaeero chori kiyer, Vitthala devalem beto

Meaning

Lord Vithoba is standing on a golden brick, in Pandharpur. I have brought a *mala* (garland) of flowers and bel for Vitthal sitting in the temple.

O Vitthal, I have brought *Pedha* and Coconut for you. The Vitthal, who helped Janabai to grind on the grinding stone is sitting in the temple.

The Vitthal, who digested the poison given to Meera bai is sitting in the temple.

The Vitthal who plucked vegetable with Savta Mali is in the temple.

The Vitthal, who made Gora Kumbhar to ram mud by foot and during whose worship he even rammed his child in the mud, that Vitthal is sitting in the temple.

O Vitthal, you always bestow your blessings on your worshippers, then we are not thieves, so why do you not bless us?

The Vitthala is sitting in the temple.

Anusuya Mata (Lord Dattatray's mother) is worshipped by them. This song is in her praise.

Anushyaa yaadee nahaalen betee
Nahaalen laaee jamburee dolee
Sigarep bal ghiyaree holee
Dattabapu hahaalen beto
Nahaaletee taayo jaamburee dolee
O moharem balee ghiyeree holee.

Meaning

Goddess Anusaya mata is taking bath.
A branch of Jamun tree has been brought for her bath.
On your (Goddess) peak a holy fire of ghee is burning.
Lord Dattatraya is also taking bath.
A branch of Jamun is also brought for his bath.
Holy fire of ghee is burning on the peak of the Mahur-God.

On festive occasions, apart from the songs pertaining to the particular festivals and Gods and Goddesses a few social songs are also sung. The followings songs indicate how the Banjara cherish bravery and think about their Banjara community and its present condition.

An Appeal to Mother for giving Birth to a Brave Son

Dharateero maandan meleeyaa
Vanshero maandan soot,
Taneree maandan tareeyaa
Baaputeero maandan poot.
Jalam des maataa
Saamant soorveer,
Nito reejo maataa vanzadee
Mat gamaav jo makhalaaro noor.
Veer des maataa saamant soor,
Parmulukhonpar kaam sadhaare.

Meaning

The earth's decoration is cloud. Similarly, a son is the decoration of a family or race. As a woman is decoration for a body (man), a son is a decoration for father. Oh, Mother, give birth to such a son who will be brave and great, or else, remain bareen, and don't lose your face. Give birth to such a brave son who will rule other countries.

Song in Praise of Banjara Community

Sab thaat padaa rah jaayegaa
Jab laad chalegaa banjaaraa
Chhod pasaaraa duniyaakaa
Vah laad chalaa hai banjaaraa
Too hai Lakkhee banjaaraa
Taanda teraa bharee hai
Gaafal dilmen mat rahana too
Bahot badaa bepaaree hai
Nammak mishree kandagiree
Faujee samaan rakhataa hai
Samsher bahaddar banjaaraa
Ganeem tujhe ghabaraataa hai

Bepaar teraa sachha hai
Aur khuda ka too hai pyaaraa
Laakh asharfee, lakkhee tole
Koun karegaa bevhaaraa
Noon gajar ka taaraa nikalaa
Banjaaran rone lagee
Banme kapatse maara gayaa
Vo naayak tha mera he dhanee
Jab anak jaakee chot padee
Rounekaa machaa hai gul saaraa
Banjaarone ga-hajab keeyaa
Samsher bhalon kaa maaraa

Meaning

The banjara marches with his goods leaving his belongings. The Tanda of Lakhu banjara is great and he should always be alert, being a big trader. The song continues praising the bravery of banjara community.

Song on the changing scenario in our country

Poro badalaayo
Suraa marderaa
Jan regee bhikaar
Aab kaaee chaleneeye faar
Jepar jor kar sarkaar
Laach lapatto vakeel khaab
Khoto karad darabaav
Dharateera upar raajkare
Ferangee baadshaahaa
Angarejaree tek saklachh
Kaanko badee malkhepar
Poro bada yo
Suraa marderaa

Meaning

Of late, the times have changed, people have become poor.
What is going on now?

The Government tries to pressurise the people. The pleaders take bribe, and all false things are accepted in the offices.

This is how the state is going on this earth.

The English sovereign and the English people have looted our country.

RITUAL SONGS

Ritual

Rituals are always a very important part of tribal life and culture. On many occasions rituals are performed for pleasing the local Gods and Goddesses or Nature like earth, trees, animals, rains etc. Thanks giving rituals are also present.

After birth of a child, while giving a name, while shaving its head, on puberty of a girl, at the time of marriage and on the death of a person rituals are performed.

Apart from such lifecycle rituals, some rituals are performed for the whole community or village. For example, the *Gaon-Bandhani* ritual of the Kolam or rituals performed for good rains in the Korku (*Bhavai*) or the rituals performed before starting for *Shikar* (hunting) and the rituals on the *Dussera* day performed by the Korkus or the Madia-Gonds are some such examples. Drinking liquor (Toddy or Mahua), dancing and singing songs are common on all such rituals.

Gondi Songs

Gondi is a dialect which is spoken by a large number of Gondi population. Many linguists consider Madia-Gondi as the original form of the dialect. However due to migration and subsequent impact of other dialects, Gondi assumed different forms in different regions and even adopted words from other languages. For example, the word *Pyāguv* from Madia (means rain) becomes Piru in Gondi while the word *Yāguv* in Madia (means water) becomes Yeru/Yer in Gondi. Let us now examine some songs from Gondi which are specimens collected from different regions of Vidarbha and parts of Madhya Pradesh.

Religious or Ritual Songs

Re Rena s s Re Rena s s Rena s s
Singar Ghatuli Pen Kela
Amot Dakom Askem Pentum Kom s s s Rena s s s Re
Nime Chouk Lihikam Baba
Nime Chouk Lihikam Mama
Gulal Bukkane Chouke Mama, Re Rena s s Re s s

Meaning

O Baba, Mama, let us worship the Singar 'Ghats' God (Pen), let us apply Gulal, Bukka etc. and worship the God. They go on adding the names of different Gods and Goddesses of the Gonds and the songs continues.

In the Gond pantheon of Gods, Lingo also called as *Pahari Kupar Lingo* occupies a prominent place. Hence a song based on Lingo worship is danced in the beginning.

Re Rena , Re Rena Re
Purrashi Kokunor Ima Tangmu Raj
Saller Jeka Niva Joka, Lingore Jeka Niva-Joka
Pulshiv Hirvanor Ima Putraj/Saller ....Lingore
Purvakot Poytar Ima Poyraj/Saller ....Lingore
Koyali Gudator Ima Modraj/Saller ....Lingore
Koya Saganor Ima Doyraj/Saller ....Lingore
Koya Punem Tor Ima Negraj/Saller ....Lingore
Sehata Pataynor Ima Legraj/Saller ....Lingore
Luski Yendaynor Ima Dakabaj/Saller ....Lingore
Maya Nalguja Tor Ima Vadiraj/Saller ....Lingore
Dholek Nangara Tor Ima Nekraj/Saller ....Lingore
Sirdi Singar Tor Ima Singraj/Saller ....Lingore
Sirdi Jeka Niva Joka, Lingore Je Ka Niva Joka.

Meaning

O God Lingo, the son of Pulshiv
Hirva we remember you and worship you and your emblem and flag (Salle).

O Lingo, the resident of Koyali Kochatgad in the republic of Purvakot and the great intelligent one who has all knowledge; the creator of the Koya (the original form of Gondi race) clans; the giver of Gondi religion, the giver and composer of our tunes, music, rhythm and dancing of the flute tunes, Dhol (drum); the one who is wise, the Sirdi Singar who plays on Nagara and Dhol, we prey you, remember you first and shout cheers in your praise.

This is the first song danced in the beginning of any ritual or dances. As stated earlier, Lingo is considered as the originator of tune, rhythm, songs and the art of dancing.

Song in Praise of Budhal Pen (Budhal God)

Māvā Budhālpen hatura rājdarbāri
Āgāda dashyā bighde, maturā kiyator dādinā
Marimar ye kamai-kiyānā, hilemāvā thikanā
Netur netur yepen kiyānā, having having Āpun tee
Niti-dharam kiyānā, agā pujā kiyānā
Māvā-Budhalpen ...1

Shetikām kiyānā, agā pujā kiyānā
Shendur pudki oyānā, kupānge ichun tāsanā
Māvā Budhalpen ...2
Undi urpāl tatānā, aden balosi tindānā
Khetikam kiyānā, agā pujā valkānā
Vajig kodā āyavel gela, pāndig kor hiyānā
Māvā Budhalpen ...3

Mava Budhalpen vehorā koyator dādina
Dopate jāvā poyānā hole kisona udānā
Sisit dalangu poyana, penku ichun hiyana
Pistal apun udana
Māvā Budhalpen ...4

Loteke āpun dayana, ālas zagdā kiyānā
Adrāmāvā Budhalpen vehorā koytor dādinā
Āgadā darshabiged matur, koytor dādinā
Māvā Budhālpen haturā rājdarbāri ...5

Meaning

My Budhal God has gone to the king's court.
Due to bad conditions there, he used to exert himself a lot.
Blood used to be offered to God, and (he) ate flesh himself.
He practised morality and religion and worshipped God.
He used to practise agriculture and used to worship God.
Vermilion and rice used to be given by him.
Then he brought a *venaris* and ate it after roasting.
He practised agriculture and worshipped God.
If paddy and kodo could not be produced (from agriculture) he used to offer pig and cock.
He used to take ambil in a pot and drink it after shaking it.
He used to take liquor in a bottle, offer a part to gods and drink the rest.
Then he used to return home and quarrel with his wife.
My Budhal God has gone to the king's court.

Mark the typical words from marathi, *e.g. raj-durbar, bighade, niti-dharma, shetikām, shendur-pudki, ālas, zagdā* etc. These words show influence of the language from neighbouring areas.

Dhemsa is a type of religious song of the Gonds and is sung by their mistrels, the Pardhans. But on the style of Dhemsa, songs on other topics are also composed and sung in a lighter vein. *Zulwa* is one of the types of such songs. Given below is a Zulwa song.

Zimur Zimur Pirwata Jadi Pirelata...
Jadi Koya Ma Bhabhi Ro Rojgya.

Manate var Motila Manate jag Motila
Zimur Zimur Pirwata, Ursa Kiya Lata
Ursa Kiya Lata Bhabhi Ro Rojgya.

Ma Nate Var Motila Ma Nate Jag Motila
Zimur Zimur Pirwata Minka Taryalat
Minek Piya Ma Bhabhi Ro Rojgya
Ma Nate Var Motila Ma Nate Jug Motila

Meaning

It is raining steadily (*Rim-Zim* or *Zimur Zimur* are onomatopoeic words for drizzling of rain), and grass is growing.

My Bhabhi (Brother's wife) is cutting grass and it is raining Rim-Zim.

Paddy saplings are to be sown, my Bhabhi is sowing paddy.

It is raining and fish are seen in the ponds; my Bhabhi is catching fish.

In Gonds also Dhemsa songs are popular. In the dances based on Dhemsa songs only men can participate, and some men put on the feminine dress and play the role of women. The reason is that in Gonds, Pardhans etc. women cannot participate in any ritual or religious function.

Lingo's Song

Mallu jandi vesad dadi
Tehra tokra mongra roye
Hachi tokra kupar
Iyam use raur ...1

Devamuku haridadi
Minukata singar dadi
Raur tale pande
Dulasta poro de dadi ...2

Pandri koko Lingo
Lingo goril Ata
Nike johar lage
Bhinda te kadurkam ...3

Nede te jilam dadi
Lingo kaldu painjena
Todi te tendune
Kavite vesoth lingo ...4

Meaning

This poem describes an imaginary temple of Lord Lingo.

Oh, Grandmother, the roof of Lingo's temple is thatched with peacock feathers, the tails of the Tehra bird are used for the border of the roof, the tails of the Hachi bird are used as channels for draining off rain water, O! my grandmother.

On all the four sides there are doors, the walls are made up from the scales of fish, within the temple is a fine bed of wool, and so is the temple Ograndmother.

In this temple is residing the younger brother of God Budhalpen, *i.e.* Lingo. In his hands is a veena which is producing delicate sounds, on his waist are tied musical bells, in his legs are painjan.

He (Lingo) is playing on a flute. From his ears music is coming out and the resonance of this music is spreading in all directions.

A Puja Song of the Madia Gonds

Beginning of any new operation is marked with a community-scale puja and dance. While sowing seeds there is a puja on the farms which is followed by a Rela and a song. One specimen song is given below:

> Bābāle bābāle, Re-reelo Ri-reelo s s s
> Ujabātti pujā Re … Re-reelo s … s
> Nārel-kāyā puja roy,
> Nimme pujā vidāstin
> Sāli metā hanumi, Re-Reelo
> Nivā khadāte vātom
> Nimme keitā vātom
> Hātek bāre Mārhiyā ... ss
> Piste bāre
> Pengād oskó vāikóm
> Nivā khadāte vāikóm, Re-Reelo s s s
> Sāli metā hanumi, Re-Reela, Rela s s s s

Meaning

Bābāle (address to all elderly persons in the village) listen. Oh, God of seeds, I am worshipping you today. I am offering coconut, incense and offering puja to you. This is a festival, which comes once in a year. I have to come to your place (on the farm). We (Madia) have come because you called us. If we die everything would be over; if we live we shall again come next year to you. Oh, God of seed-grains, we have come to you, as this is a festival which comes once in a year.

Ritual Songs of the Kolam

Like many other tribal communities, the Kolam also have ritual songs. They have traditional folk-songs which are sung on such occasions. A few songs are given below:

While worshipping deities, songs in praise of Gods and Goddesses are sung which can be classified as *Pooja* (worship) Songs.

A Pooja Song

Rena Rena Re Rena, Rena Rena Re
Ura Devi Ennive Devi
Innung Narel –Shendur
Ura Bhimayak Ennive Bhimayak
Inung Pillu Pichuk
Ura Jayatur Ennive Jayatur
Inung Tuke Urmakad
Ura Maroti Ennive Maroti
Inung Beli Phutane
Ura Marayak Ennive Marayak
Inung Nalapuliye

This is a song for performing the *Puja* of Gods and Goddesses. O Goddess you are our mother and we are your children. We offer a coconut and *sindur* to you. You bless us.

O God Bhimayak we offer a chicken to you.
O God Jaytur we offer the dish which you like very much.
O God Maroti we offer jaggery and fried grams to you.
O God Marayak we offer the vegetable which you like most.
O Gods bless us all.

Another Pooja Song

Re Rena Re Rena
Indi Yena diyalakung diyal Yena Wattev
Bara Meyane Nav Yend Tapnat Wattev
Diyalung Yena Shendur, Bukka Siyur
Ral Gi, Kisiktana Kapur Yena Siyyur

Soni ani Paiku Sukhi Dukhanet Veltorur yeta
Yendet Iyyeltad Pik-Pani Yanang aad Yena
Podilav Sebbungsathi Taned lagave Yena
Muttung Yendug Ovvol Yedad Payajen Yena

Meaning

This song is in praise of God.

O God you come and bless us throughout twelve months. We offer you *Shendur, Bukka, Siyur Ral,* ignited *Kapur*. We also offer you money and all other things. You give us happiness and take away our pains. Let our crops grow well.

This song is sung at the time of the worship of traditional Gods.

Pooja Song — Oora Devi Song

Rena Rena Re Rena, Rena Rena Re
Ware Ware Oora Devi
Aame Watume Alange
Aame Watume Alange
Kay Kiyya Sukhame Apeye
Ware Ware Bhimayak Diyyam
Aame Watume Alange
Aame Watume Sukhame Apeye
Ware Ware Jeyatur Diyyam
Aame Watume Alange, Jeyatur
Kal – Kiyya Sukhame Apeye
Ware Ware Amma Diyyam
Aame Watume Alange
Aame Watume Amma Diyyam
Kal – Kiyya Sukhaya Apeye.

Meaning

The tribal people worship the Moon, the Sun and other objects from nature.

"Oh, Goddess Oora Devi, we have come to you, please bless us.

Oh, God Bhimayak you please bless us.
Oh, God Jeyatur please come and bless us.
Oh, Goddess "Aamma" you please come and bless us.

We are all like your children so forgive our mistakes.

This song is also in praise of clan Gods like Ghettalal, Pikkalal etc.

Rena Rena Re Rena Re
Annete Marge Ghettalal Pejite
Ghettalal Pejite
Annete Marge Pikkalal Pejite
Pikkalal Pejite
Annete Marge Tongenal Pejite
Tongenal Pejite
Annete Marge Tikanenal Pejite
Tikanenal Pejite
Annete Marge Arulinal Pejite
Arulinal Pejite
Annete Marge Tallal Pejite
Tallal Pejite
Annete Marge Susulival Pejite
Sunsulival Pejite.

Oh, God Ghettalal we offer you Pooja so that you will pardon us for our mistakes. Some of us have ailments in body. Some have problems with knees or legs. Some have fever while other suffer from headache or bodyache. Some have lost their parents while some have lost their children. Some are about to die. This means that all have committed mistake. So we are worshipping God Pikkalal, Tongenal, Arulinal, Tallal and Susulival.

The function of *Gaon-Bandhani* is an important ritual. The village is fortified against all evil things and bad omen by this ritual. The following songs are sung during this ritual.

In praise of the Goddess at *Mahur*:

Mahurta Devi Tandung Wattina
Tandung Toda?
Bara Menela Punja

Tineng Wattin! ...1
Mahurta Polegama Tandung Wattina
Tandung Toda ?
Bara Menela Punja
Tineng Wattin ! ...2
Mahurta Polegama Uddeng Suleng Tang
Anang Kada Tang Toda?
Bara Menela Khushi
Kakeng Battin! ...3
Aaura Pillakul Iyura Pillakul
Tadung Kultera Tadung Toda?
Satti Oleng Wattev!

Meaning

O Mahur Goddess why have you come? And for what have you not come?
For accepting twelve months Puja!
O Polegama from Mahur why have you come?
For accepting twelve months Puja!
O Polegama from Mahur
Why are you standing up and sitting down?
For enjoying the happiness, pleasure for twelve months.
Women and girls from that town and children from our town have come together,
for what purpose?
To see the ceremony of "Gaon Bandhani"!

Korku Ritual Songs

Birthday Songs

Charkhut, Char bhavan
Rama Thakur rekha dale
Pancho mahine ka loi
Nau mahine ke balak
Sone ki thali
Ange dhulaya ...1

Sone ke zula zulaya
Aankh ke diya, hath ke palana
Our godi ki palki
Zula Zulaya ...2
Tere mane mishri Dudh Pilayi
Ga, ga, geet sunai
Zula zulaya ...3

Meaning

O child, Rama Thakur (Shri Rama) has given you life. In the fifth month you got blood, in the ninth month you came to this world. Mother gave you bath in golden tub and gave golden cradle for sleeping. Her eyes were the lights (kept vigil on you) and hands became your palanquin. She gave milk with mishri (sugar crystals) and she sung songs for you.

Eh, dossoni, Eh dostin
Aamni do s s do s s
Cholaj ghar aave
Aamne do s s do s s ...1
Eh, Maina, Eh Maina
Ja beta
Aamne do s s do ...2
Ghar laya tere Roke re
Aamne do s s do s s ...3

Meaning

A lulling song to silence the child which has less of meaning but more of rhythm. (O friend, O maina please go, the child is crying etc.)

Lulling Song

Gai dodure, Gai dodure
  Beta soja re
  Rona nai.
Gai dodure, Gai dodure,
  Beta soja re

Rona nai.
Mayo aayee re
Rona nai
Bapo aaya re
Rona nai
Maya aaya re
Dudhu layo re
Rona nai.

Meaning

Child don't cry, sleep. Your mother is bringing cow milk for you. Your father has come, your mother has come. Don't cry, sleep.

Ama re baba,
Sage ba takra Ro .... Ro .... Ro .... Ro ....
Katam ko boko
Katam ko boko
Ro .... To .... Ro

Meaning

A rhythmic song for lulling children in cradle. The words are changed as per fancy.

Sidoli Songs

Sidoli or *Phuljajni* is a ritual for giving solace to a departed soul. Vulgar words and abuses in these songs are meant to please the soul.

The elder men and women dance and sing.
The Males say —

Helere aama do do gande
Sana lagito do do gande ...1

Meaning

The terms used are vulgar and straightaway refer to male and female genital organs and hint of intercourse.

The Women say —
Guinama murda muaar
Aam rongo konde muaar ebe hona

The partner is of morose face. His face is black as if burnt. These are vulgar questions and answers full of abuses and sex acts – only elderly and married women participate. (Girls don't participate in it.)

Raja Rutu Jamaikula (Kui s s)
Raja Ram[illegible] Jamaikula (Kui s s s)
Raja Lootmare Zagda sunai (Kui s s s)

These are also vulgar words addressed by women to men during the dance sequence.

Khamm

Khamm is a ritualistic dance-drama performed from Ganesh festival (*Bhadrapad Chaturthi* to *Anant Chaturdashi*) and may be performed up to *Kartik Ekadashi*. However, if some took religious vow it may be performed any time up to *Ekadashi* or during *Diwali* festival.

A wooden post (Kham or Khamb) is erected at the centre and on its upper end is fixed a wheel of bullock-cart. This structure represents the *Sudarshan Chakra* of Lord Krishna. Only men participate in this dance. Men put on *sarees* and perform the role of women. Songs regarding Rama-Laxman are also sung during this dance. Two groups participate in dancing and while one group initiates, the other follows it. To start with they are in the *Vilambit laya* (slow pace) and then they pass on to *Drut laya* (fast pace). The songs are mostly based on Lord Krishna but names of Lord Ganesh, Lord Mahadeva, Goddess Parbati also follow:

Wari Wari Wari Mera Ganpati Deva,
Wari Wari Wari Mera Ganpati Deva

Pahale manao Ganrajko,
Wari Wari Wari Mera Ganpati Deva . . . 1

Mata teri Parvati, Pita Mahadeva,
Wari Wari Wari Mera Ganpati Deva . . . 2

(O! Lord Ganpati, you are great and I worship you first. Your mother is Parvati and father is Lord Mahadeva and we worship them.

O, Lord Ganesh you are great.)

They go on adding names of deities and can go on singing for any length of time.

***Muthwa* Puja**

It is the local deity at the centre of every village and they first offer *Puja, i.e.* worship this God. Other deities are also worshipped and prayed in songs.

Hath jode re woke paya palore Ram
Mathura Nangar Suwano Lal
Sab devtanse Muthwa balore Ram
Mathura Nangar ...
Sab devatanse khalkya balore Ram
Mathura Nangar ...
Hath jode re woke paya palore Ram
Sab devatanse Devi balore Ram
Mathura Nangar ...
Sab devatanse Mahadeo balore Ram
Mathura Nangar ...
Hath jode re, woke paya palore
Mathura Nangar Suwane Lal.

Thus, this song is in praise and prayer of Muthwa Deo, Mahavir, Khalkya, Devi and Mahadeo – the different deities worshipped by them. O God, I bow down before you with folded hands and you are greater than all other Gods. This line is repeated substituting the names of Gods.

There are songs praising the *Bhumka* who worships Gods for the community.

Bhumkari Bhumkari
Kharik, Limbu Pujanwalo Bhumkari
Bhumkari, Nariyal, Sindur, Pujnewalo Bhumkari
Bhumkari, Kajal, Kunku, Pujnewalo Bhumkari
Bhumkari, Murgi, Bakra, Pujnewalo Bhumkari
Bhumkari, Daru, Khichda, Pujnewalo Bhumkari

In this song the Bhumka or the priest who performs *puja* with various articles like coconut, *Sindur* (Vermilion), *Kumkum*, cock, he-goat, liquor, *khichdi* (a mixed recipe) is praised.

Aarti of King Ravana

Chojama Aarti do
Raja Ravana ke Aarati Le
Sone ke Aarti Bai
Rupe ki Bari Bai
Rupe ki Bari Bai
Raja Ravana ke Aarti Le

Ye Sali Ko sadi de
Bai Hira moti Perile
Hera Moti Perile
Raja Ravana ke Aarti Le

Aarti Ma Aarti Bai
Chojama Aarti do
Chojama Aarti do
Raja Ravana ke Aarti Le

O, lady (Bai) whose *Aarti* are you doing? The lady tells that it is King Ravana's *Aarti*. The *Aarti* is of Gold and the wick, is of silver, the lady has put on new *sari* and has diamonds on her body; and this lady is performing *Aarti* of King Ravana.

Korkus are worshippers of King Ravana and though they now worship the other Hindu Gods, this *Aarti* testifies to their original links with distant past.

Ravana Song – Dussera Day

Lanka Ravani Jugi tau ten Olen Joy
Lanka Ravani Jugi tau ten olen ...1
Lanka Ravana Jugi Jodama Doyana Joy
Lanka Ravana Jugi tan ten olen ...2
Lanka Ravana tika Thenga Doyana Joy
Lanka Ravana tau ten olen ...3
Lanka Ravana Chunuka Chingi Doyana Joy
Lanka Ravana tau ten olen ...4

Lanka Ravana danda Zuli Doyana Joy
Lanka Ravana Jugi tau ten olen ...5

Rawana came with *Danda, Punji, Painjan, Jholi* and *Tika* and looked very impressive as a *Jogi*, and being fascinated towards his personality 'she' went along with him. (Who is 'She' is everybody's guess work!)

This song sung on the Dussehra day very much establishes their faith in King Ravana of Lanka whom they traditionally consider as their ancestor (*Ravan-banshi*) and King.

Bhavai is an important ritual of the Korku. They please the rain God by celebrating *Rand Bhave* and after the first showers of rain celebrate *Chikla-Bhave* as if to thank the rain God. Following two songs are sung while dancing on the occasion.

Rand Bhave

Dedera mata pani de
Pani de
Serom Serom, Serom Serom
Jwarpala suki gayo re
Pani de, Pani de . . . 1
Serom Serom, Serom Serom
Dedara mata Pani de
Pani de . . . 2
Rand bhave ye je ba lambe ko
Chikla bhave ye je ba lambe ko
Kodki kele lambe ko
Kutki Khede lambe ko
Chikla bhave ye je ba lambe ko. . . . 3

We pray Dedera Goddess for giving water (rains) as the *Jaur* crops have dried. Give us water. We are just surviving on *Kutki* (a minor millet).

Young boys and children also dance with elders and move in the village with an earthen pot filled with water and covered with Neem and other leaves. A frog (considered as a sign of rain-God) is kept in the pot.

After showers of rain there is *Chikla* (mud mixed with water)

Bhave to celebrate joy and to thank the rain God. They sing the following song.

Chikla Bhave

Potti Khede tu yeba
to ye ba manaile
Chikla bhave ye jeba
Ye jeba manaile . . . 1
Baba Kade to yeba
To ye ba manaile . . . 2
Chikla bhave ye jeba
Ye jeba manaile . . . 3

We are celebrating *Chikla Bhave* in our village, so you come for celebrating it.

Ritual Songs of the Banjara

On the birth of a child a ritual called *Natalo* is performed before Holi. On that day this song is sung.

Pelo naam swamoree le syan
Swameero jaayo aanand badayo
Dusaroye naam mahelyaaro le syan
Mahelyaaro jaayo aanand badaayo
Tisaroye naam dharatiyo re syan
Dhartiro jaayo aanand vadaayo

Too bhalo jalmeeyo kesareeya Rajpoot
Taare aangan galras aamblo
Too bhalo jalmeeye arjun sareekhe bir
Taare aangan galras aamblo
Too bhalo jalmeeye raavaleeyaake Rajpoot
Taare aangan galras aambalo

Meaning

Prayer is offered to Gods like Swami, Mallhar (Shiva), the earth, and then, the child is called with the names of heroic persons like Kesariya

Rajput, Arjun, Ravaliya Rajput, etc. and offered blessings. This song is mostly sung by women.

A Lulling Song

Zujeebaalaa zujoore, gogo tuk topodoo
Zija sidaadoo hasrooro bag lagaadoo kelaaro
Haatem daandiyaa sonero, baalaa sojor
Halo karook paalo karoo, baalaa rov jetee kaso karoo ...1
Haaroor gular khotvaadee, baalaa suto zudpaadee
Taar thaadee geech haaten, laale kaachaa kodee
Baalaa so jor
Halo baabaa Halo dhoroomaaee chaalo suko daalyaa khaalo
Kulbyaaree bhandee maadee, taare gharet sankaadee ...2

Meaning

O'child sleep in the cradle, shall I give you jaggery or coconut. Shall I stitch a shirt for you or plant a garden of bananas for you? I shall put a gold ring on your hand, please sleep.

I am rocking your cradle for long but you are not sleeping, so what shall I do?

Your mother has kept you on the farm and has gone to bazaar, and she will bring a kavadi (shell) for you wheat flour, please sleep.

The house of Kunbis are well built (Madi) but you are under thatched roof, so please sleep.

Lulling Song

Haalo haalo karagee zoleem savaargee
Kaee dago degree baalen baaee ye
Naamdev baalaa galeetee kar chaalaaye
Mare baalen jijaan topeeye
Toee maaro baalaa samjenee baaeeye ...1
Taare baalaan dudheree kayoleeye
Toee taro baalo samjenee baaeeye
Adoshee padosheer najar laageechye
Nul marchyaaree najar kadaaeeye
Toee taro baalaa samjenee baaeeye

Soner chendoo chandeer daando haatem
Toee taro baalaa samjenee baaeeye ...2

Meaning

Child's mother rocked the cradle and went away to the farm missing his eye. Namdeo bal (another child by name Namdeo) plays in the street, and my child has a shirt and cap (purporting to say that Namdeo has not), even then why my child is crying. I don't understand.

I have given milk to your child in a bowl. I don't understand why your child is still crying?

I thought that bad looks of neighbours have affected you, I used salt and chillies to remove the bad effect of the 'look' (Drishta, *i.e.* Najar), even then your child is crying.

Your child has got a ball of gold and has a silver ring on wrist, even then the child does not stop crying.

While sowing seeds this song is sung.

Jalman kaaee kamaaee maaree maatąaye
Pąan phool vaace gamaaceye
Vor aastureen lataay kapadaa
Maataan cheetaree vitaaye
Voree astureen ghodep basaaro
Maataan paidal chalaaye
Aangeshee malgoye eknaraashee
Ghod-lep berovaalo kulaye
Ghodlep besévaalee or aasturee
Paidar chaalevaalee maataaye
Voree maataan seelepaale takdaaye
Voree aastureen shiraan puree.

Meaning

By giving birth what could mother earn? Leaves and flowers are wasted. The wife gets a new cloth while a mother gets torn pieces of cloth. His wife gets a horse to ride while mother walks on foot. While walking he met a man who asked, "who is sitting on the horse?" Reply came that the horse rider was his wife while the pedestrian was his mother. Stale food for the mother and sweets to wife.

Another sowing song

Baaeeye soyak guleero padeye dhado mandoch
Katven padeeye chor
Baaeeye dhade hundyaang tokalo padoch
Baaeeye tokler upar vatalaa padoch
Vataalaar upar zaaree padoch
Zaareere upar ganlo padoch
Katven padeeye chor
Baaeeye tokler hundyang bhaalaa gadoch
Katven padeeye chor
Baaeeye bhalaatee aaboo zaaboo bandech
Katven padeeye chor

Meaning

Oh sister, a pandal of strong mat (Bamboo mat) or canvass is constructed, how can a thief enter? Oh sister, a big utensil (Gund) has been kept and on it is placed Zari (a big spoon) and a disc is placed on its mouth. How can a thief come? Near the utensil is kept a javelin and two dogs are sitting near it. How can a thief come?

Sant Janabai, a Marathi Saint is worshipped by them. When the women grind grain on grinding stone they sing this song.

Janaabaaeen ghatee pisanye
Kaaee ton bhakteeree godeer Vithobaa
Bheem – Arjuneree jodeer Vithobaa
Janaabaaeer dhondo dhoyachee
Jan vataalo konee aayor Vithobaa
Kaaee ton bhakteeree godeer Vithobaa
Bheem – Arjaneree jodeer Vithobaa
Janaabaaeer sadaa naakehee
Janaa kataalo konee aagov Vithobaa
Kaaee ton bhakteeree godeer Vithobaa
Bheem – Arjuneree jodeer Vithobaa.

Meaning

O God Vithoba, you helped Janabai in grinding grain. How sweet is your Bhakti (worship). As if Bhim and Arjun who were inseparable brothers.

You helped Janabai in washing clothes but were not tired, how sweet is your Bhakti.

You sprinkled water in the courtyard of Janabai but were not tired, how sweet is your Bhakti? As if the inseparable brothers Bhim and Arjun.

O Vithoba, your love for your worshipper (here Janabai) can be compared to the close brotherhood of Bhim and Arjuna.

4

Conclusion

The overview of tribal folk literature which is taken in the preceding pages shows that it is replete with literary styles and figures of speech. If we examinate from a literary point of view the language or rather the words used are natural but full of figurative literary styles and moreover can be sung with rhythm. In fact singing a poem is a peculiarity of tribal poetry because for oral transmission this was essential. These songs are not only sung but are collectively sung and that to while dancing. Hence, the above two characteristics become necessary.

Tribal songs contain various human sentiments which may include amorous love and affection, affection for child, brother-sister affection, bravery, humour, teasing etc. But the most favourite subject is regarding Gods and Goddesses, spirituality, origin of earth and mankind, intricacies of nature etc. The local Gods and Goddesses and the clan Gods take priority over other Gods. Those forces of nature which are queer also occupy a large part of the subject matter. It is also seen that though they are worshippers of their tribal deities, they have also adopted worship of Gods and incarnations from the other cultural streams living in India, *e.g.* Shriram, Shrikrishna (also Vitthal), Hanuman and even many saints are the subject of the worship-songs. In some tribes like the Korku even Ravan, Meghnad and Kumbhakarna are worshipped and described in their songs.

Nature is one of the main inspiration and also a subject matter of many songs. Sun and Moon, Earth, Trees, Animals and Birds are described or referred to in many songs. But out of these some are the signs of their totem. Such animals or trees get priority as subjects for songs.

Lulling songs are typical in their style and may be compared fairly well with those in the advanced modern literature. The arrangement of words and the singing style/meter is also befitting.

Many social and economic aspects and issues are also reflected in the songs, *e.g.* – poverty and richness, market and marketing, bride-price, the condition of tribals, are some of the issues which find place in their songs. Praise of their Chief/Patel or King and also of the brave deeds of past leaders of their tribes are described in many songs.

Relationship between the spouses and amorous between the lover and his beloved are profuse with different ideas, figurative language, imagination and styles. Many such songs are sung on marriage occasions or on some festive occasions. A typical feature of these songs is, they may contain abuses and even words indicating sex and sexual relationships. This is a method of sublimating these ideas from the mind of persons and converting them into a social entertainment which is very pure and simple. Due to this, perversions can be avoided. One must also remember that steady growth of the race is also an important necessity of tribal society and from this point of view their culture has considered sex as a basic necessity of their community.

The various figures of speech commonly used are alliteration, metaphors and simile.

In some poems even transferred epithets are used and all these things are very natural and that too composed by persons who are illiterate. Most of the tribals are, by nature, quick poets. They compose songs or may change the subject matter of songs on the spur of the moment so as to suit the occasion. e.g. – To welcome a guest or to describe modern education, elections, development etc...Their talents have produced songs based on these new themes.

Tribal folk theatre also represents a combination of dance-songs and the performing art. For example – The Dandhar continues for hours together and the themes also go on changing. The costumes, instruments and the make-up used on such occasion are conceived by them and prepared mostly from indigenous and locally available material. Moreover they have kept intact the marks of ancient Indian culture which they inherited for the last two thousand years or so.

AN UNDERCURRENT OF UNITY IN FOLK LITERATURE

The folk literature of different tribes presents some similarities and some dissimilarities. Usually the tribes from the same ethnic groups show similarities, *e.g.* the Gonds including the Madia Gonds, Kolam, Pardhan are from Dravidian group. On the other hand the Korku are from the Munda or Kaularian ethnic group. The Banjara, though a nomadic tribe is originally from the Rajputana side. The Korku are also culturally nearer to the Banjaras, the Bhils, Warli, Thakar tribes. Hence, there are some similarities in their folk literature.

Though the Madia, the Kolam and the Katkari are classified as primitive tribes, their habitat, ethnic background etc. is different. Hence, there are many differences in their folklore.

However, the sentiments, emotions, oneness with nature, social attitude and community spirit etc. are almost the same. Their rituals and ceremonies, for celebrating birth, death, marriage and other festivals are much similar although the details, may vary. The mother-earth and nature surrounding them are always objects of worship and a sense of gratitude is expressed towards them through the songs or tales. In many tribes the stories related to the creation of mankind are similar and indicate that man was created from earth and as such after death is reborn on the earth. On the whole, one can easily conclude that in spite of differences in their ethnic origin, dialects and some other aspects of life, the undercurrent of tribal culture is the same for all these tribes.

Marriage Songs

These songs form a very significant and popular portion of tribal folk songs. The bride's party and the groom's party come together for the marriage ceremony and these songs are sung either by the women from both the parties or alternately like question-answer sessions. These include subjects like praise of the bride and finding faults with the grooms. Harassing the other party, bride price, the painful feelings due to parting of the daughter etc. Of course, the emphasis on subject matter varies according to its importance in the tribe. For example applying turmeric powder to the body of the bride is described in many marriage songs in different tribes. Same can be said about the songs for giving send-off to the bride. In some tribes they have adopted some rituals from the non-tribals surrounding them. Hence, different subjects find place in their songs. The Madia marriage songs profusely describe the custom of bride price. Similarly their songs describing the separation of their daughter from her parents are very poignant and touching. Humour, slang comments and teasing are very common in many marriage songs. The groom's sister-in-law (*sali*) is often the subject matter of such songs.

Spiritual Songs

The tribals live a simple life which obviously is materialistic in nature, but traditionally they love songs which emphasise spiritualism and advocate reducing the wants and turning to worship of Gods and Saints. Such songs are available in all tribes but more so in the Kolam and the Banjara in the present collection. These should not be confused with the worship songs sung at the time of worshipping Gods. They are ritualistic in nature, but the spiritual songs try to divert the attention of men and women to that invisible and unknown spirit which is the ultimate truth.

After going through the foregoing pages the reader will get some idea of the performing art of the tribal communities and its relation with folk literature. It is all pure, simple, spontaneous and indigenous in nature. The classicism seen in their songs is not a product of scholarship but a natural response of human heart and mind to the environmental and social interaction. This accounts for the unity in culture.

Bibliography

Deogaonkar, S.G., (1982), *The Madia of Bhamragad*, New Delhi, Inter-India Publications.

Deogaonkar, S.G., Deogaonkar, Shailaja, S., (1990), *The Korku Tribals*, New Delhi, Concept Publishing Company.

Deogaonkar, S.G., Deogaonkar, Shailaja, S., (1990), *Madia Gondanchi Boli*, Mumbai, Maharashtra Rajya Sahitya Sanskriti Mandal.

Deogaonkar, S.G., Deogaonkar, Shailaja, S., (1992), *The Banjara*, New Delhi, Concept Publishing Company.

Deogaonkar, Shailaja, S., (1993), *Maharashtratil Adiwasinche Lok Sahitya*, Nagpur, Shri Sainath Prakashan.

Murkute, S.R., (1991), *Socio-cultural Study of Scheduled Tribe: The Pradhan of Maharashtra*, New Delhi, Concept Publishing Company.

Patil, Baliram, Hiraman, (1936), *Gor-Banjara Lokancha-Itihas*, Yavatmal, B.M. Patil Smarak Samiti.

Russel, R.V., Hiralal, (1975), *Tribes and Castes of the Central Provinces of India*, Vol. II, New Delhi, Cosmo Publications.

INDEX